Sacred Feathers

The Power of One Feather to Change Your Life

By
Maril Crabtree

Adams Media Corporation
Avon, Massachusetts

Published by
Adams Media Corporation
57 Littlefield Street
Avon, MA. 02322. U.S.A.

www.adamsmedia.com

ISBN: 1-58062-707-2

Printed in Canada.

J I H G F E D C B

Library of Congress Cataloging-in-Publication Data
Sacred feathers : the power of one feather to change your life / [edited] by Maril
Crabtree.
p. cm.
ISBN 1-58062-707-2
1. Feathers—Miscelleanea. I. Crabtree, Maril.

BF1999 .S245 2002
291.3'7—dc21

2002074482

This publication is designed to provide accurate and authoritative information with regard to the subject matter covered. It is sold with the understanding that the publisher is not engaged in rendering legal, accounting,
or other professional advice. If legal advice or other expert assistance is
required, the services of a competent professional person should be sought.
—From a *Declaration of Principles* jointly adopted by a
Committee of the American Bar Association and
a Committee of Publishers and Associations

Cover and interior photograph by ©Chris Collins/The Stock Market.

This book is available at quantity discounts for bulk purchases.
For information, call 1-800-872-5627.

This book is dedicated to:

Virginia Lenore Briand Crabtree, my mother-in-law,

whose life has inspired and affirmed me as

much as my beloved feathers have.

Permissions

Contents

PART TWO
The Power of Feathers:
Messages of Healing and Transformation

PART THREE

Light as a Feather:
Messages of Freedom, Surrender, and Letting Go

PART FOUR

Where There's a Quill, There's a Way!
Messages of Love, Strength, and Courage

Acknowledgments

I WOULD LIKE TO ACKNOWLEDGE MY HUSBAND, Jim, whose support has been a constant healing presence; my daughter Virginia, daughter-in-law Tiffany, son Jim, sister Sandy, and Gloria, who have been fountains of support and encouragement; my housemates and chosen partners in life, Bill Grover, Judith Christy, and Bob Mann, who saw me through all stages and phases of this endeavor; my dear friend Deborah Shouse, without whose support, advice, and wisdom there simply would be no book; my spiritual partners in addition to those named above, Ron Zoglin, Robert Brumet, Stan Leutung, Roberta Vogel, Helen and Ron Yeomans, Patti Cawthon, Warren and Cheryl Varney, Sharil Baxter, and Paulla Levitch; my editor, Claire Gerus, who has been a mentor throughout the entire process of producing this book; my Naples writing partners Liz, Sissel, Pauline, Nancy, Barbara, and Peggy, and all of the members of the Kansas City Writers Group who cheered me on through the rollercoaster ride of first-time authorship; Mark Carr, Cate Cummings, Denise Linn, Victoria Moran, and Saphira, whose early encouragement and support were much appreciated; and all the contributors of the sacred stories in this book, many of whom are now cherished friends because of what they shared.

Prologue

A FEW YEARS AGO, I WALKED THE STREETS OF Aspen, Colorado, feeling nothing but darkness despite the bright sunlight. I had just ended three years of directing a fledgling nonprofit organization, working fourteen-hour days to help low-income people. Filled with stress and every negative emotion you can imagine, I felt burned out. The future loomed like a huge blank wall, as insurmountable as the mountains surrounding me on all sides. I panicked at the very thought of what to do next.

For more than four decades, I had "progressed" from achievement to achievement. With my inner hunger for recognition, I had excelled in everything. I swallowed whole careers and moved on: first, teaching; then, mothering; next, getting a law degree; working for a law firm; practicing law on my own; working with the poor. Nothing satisfied my inner restlessness. Nothing was "proof" enough that I was a worthy human being. What was left?

As I paused for breath after walking uphill, something directed my attention to my feet. Directly in front of me lay an immense shiny feather. I stared at it. Where had it come from? I looked overhead. No birds in sight. Just the feather and me. I heard a voice inside: "Go ahead and pick it up. It's for you. You are not alone, you know."

The feather was smooth, silky, and black. Was

it my imagination that made it seem to glow with an inner light? I picked it up and held it in both hands. From somewhere inside me, the voice spoke even more distinctly: "You are loved. You are an integral part of this vast web of interconnection. You are not alone."

I continued to hold the feather reverently. A sense of gratitude and joy filled me. This beautiful black messenger from the sky had fully answered my black thoughts about being in an empty universe. I later learned that in many ancient traditions a black feather is a sign of mystical wisdom received from spiritual initiation. Such feathers (from crows, ravens, or starlings) are often worn by shaman figures. The large black feather awaiting me in Aspen provided my own initiation into the wisdom of the universe.

I kept that black feather. Each time I hold it, its powerful message comes through: *You are not alone. We are with you; all of life is part of you. Fly with the wind!*

Introduction

I am a feather on the bright sky
I am the blue horse that runs in the plain
I am the fish that rolls, shining, in the water. . . .
You see, I am alive, I am alive.
            —N. Scott Momaday,
            The Delight Song of Tsoai-Talee

FEATHERS! MAGICAL, MYSTICAL, INCREDIBLE feathers! Feathers of all shapes, sizes, varieties, and colors. Throughout history, feathers have served as spiritual symbols for shamans and priests, as symbols of royalty for kings and chiefs, as symbols of healing, or as symbols of sacred power for cultures as far back as the ancient Egyptian, Asian, or Celtic eras. These cultures possessed abilities to communicate with nature in ways that have been overlooked or forgotten in our own time.

Yet feathers are more than history. For many, they are mystical signs, messages, or opportunities. They are scraps of synchronicity in the flowing patchwork of universal meanings. Feathers appear in unlikely places as assurances of well being, as a comforting sign of abundance in the universe, and as unmistakable messengers of hope and encouragement. Their ephemeral grace makes them the perfect emissaries of spiritual and emotional freedom.

For the past three years, I have been guided to collect true stories from people whose lives have been changed because of feathers: feathers as sacred messengers, as conduits to enlightenment, as harbingers of inner truth, or as gentle reminders of a synchronistic and abundant universe. These stories are powerful accounts of how feathers teach, guide, and inspire us. They offer true examples of how the universe speaks to us through an "ordinary" but mystical object—a feather.

How can a feather—an inanimate object—speak to us? How can we receive messages from part of a bird's wing? What is it about feathers—as opposed to coffee cups or quilts or wildflowers—that qualifies them to be harbingers of universal truth?

We live in a holographic cosmos, where a piece of the whole reflects the entire whole. When a feather leaves its bird-home and falls to earth, it carries all of the energy of its former attachment to a living being. From a cosmic perspective, the feather also carries within it, as we carry within ourselves, the universal energy we call by many names, from "God" to "Spirit" to "divine life force." Why not, then, accept that this feather falls into our lives to give us a message directly from that life force?

When I see a feather lying in an unexpected place, or even in a usual place but noticed only by me among the hundreds who have passed by, I know it is meant for me. Not every feather is "special" nor is every piece of stone or every crystal.

But the potential for connection is there. I need only to listen from that open-hearted space inside me that urges me to soar higher. I need only to acknowledge that, as one storyteller put it, "there are simple powers, strange and real" that affect me.

Feathers also have universal symbolic meanings, recognized by tribes and traditions worldwide. Feathers speak to us of flight, of freedom, of going beyond boundaries, of getting "above it all," of the need to let go and travel light. In many cultures, feathers carried prayers to heavenly gods and bestowed extraordinary powers in battle.

Above all, feathers come to us as gifts. They come from the sky, from the sea, from trees and deep grasses, even from—as these stories illustrate—enclosed spaces never inhabited by winged creatures. They come to us unexpectedly but not without purpose. Their messages may be startling, soothing, or sudden, but they are always an opportunity for seeing—for finding answers to questions we may not even have known we were asking.

What, then, is a feather? It is a part of a bird's body, and it is a part of us. It exists for itself, to serve its primary purpose in the cosmos, and it exists in alliance with every other aspect of the cosmos. Just as we bring life-inspiring messages for others while simply fulfilling our own lives, so feathers bring their messages to us. They remind us that we walk in a world overflowing with meaning.

This book contains my own feather stories and the experiences of others. In each, there is some bud of wisdom or truth gained from an encounter with feathers. These stories are offered as gifts for your own life journey and as evidence that the universe speaks to us in many ways.

You'll also find suggestions for ways to explore the feather connections in *your* life, from attracting feathers for your own collection to using feathers in a variety of ceremonies, meditations, and rituals.

Feathers will teach us many things if we are ready to learn. Linda Hogan, whose miraculous story "The Feathers" is included in this book, reminds us that there is "something alive in a feather. . . . It knows the insides of clouds. It carries our needs and desires, the stories of our brokenness."

The feather stories you read here will confirm that feathers heal our wounds, lead us to newfound freedom, help us surrender to a joyful universe, and create a powerful sense of connection with all that is beyond the rational intellect. Feathers carry us into the soul's most intimate places, where we find our own wings to climb higher than ever before.

Part One

The Mystery of Feathers:

Mystical Messages

from the Spirit

You Can Do It!

Maril Crabtree

MY FEET ARE ON FIRE. THE ASPHALT HIGHWAY stretches before me, no end in sight. It is hot— more than hot: it is steaming, a typical hot, muggy August day in eastern Missouri. The only wind comes from passing eighteen-wheelers, and that wind feels like someone opened the oven door and fanned the heat straight at me.

I have been walking for hours, since early morning, and it's three in the afternoon, the hottest part of the day. I wipe the sweat off my face and feel the smear of sunblock as it drips off my chin. My hair is wet and matted under my brimmed hat. My calves hurt, my hips are tender, and every bone and muscle in my body screams at me to stop.

I am familiar with this pain. I have done this before. Every year for several years now, between August 6 and August 9, I and a few others have put one foot in front of the other for 63 miles' worth of highway, each footstep representing a Japanese civilian killed in the Hiroshima-Nagasaki atomic bombings. This year twenty of us are walking, a small band of peace pilgrims remembering the anniversary of that terrible tragedy, of a world of pain and hurt far greater than the world of my body, a world at war. We ended that war only to begin another: the war for nuclear "defense," for "security" through nuclear weapons. Each year, I walk across this Missouri farmland still pocked with missile silos to remind myself that I have a choice, a choice about my own life, and what I can do for peace.

But now I am about to give up. The longest hill of the entire journey lies before me and I have a mile to go before the top, where I can have a blessed drink of water and a ten-minute rest. I have fallen behind everyone else; I don't dare stop before I reach the top of the hill. But I don't see how I can make it. My eyes blur with sweat and pain.

Then I see the feather: large, pristine, perfectly white, waving at me from the grassy meadow beside the highway shoulder. Why haven't all the huge trucks passing blown it away? I'll never know, but the feather persists, gently waving at me and saying, as plainly as if it had shouted the words into my ears, "You can do it!"

And I laugh, knowing I *can*. I feel new energy from the feather pouring into my body, as if it has given me wings of pure light. I almost run the mile up that hill, bursting with laughter and light. I am a bird flying up the hill, flapping my wings with joy, no longer exhausted but exhilarated. This hill will never again be an insurmountable challenge.

Another thought soars into my consciousness. If I can fly up that hill, I can do anything! I have only to tap into the limitless energy of the universe that always surrounds us and I can be instantly renewed. All the next day, the memory of that pure white feather glows in my mind, and it feeds my tired muscles through the final miles of our walk.

When I returned home, I tried to identify the kind of bird that might have left such a feather in the middle of a Missouri field. No one could tell me. Was I hallucinating? It didn't matter. I knew that the energy I received was no hallucination, and I knew I could climb any literal or figurative hill . . . with a little help from my winged friends. 🖋

The Feathers

Linda Hogan

FOR YEARS I PRAYED FOR AN EAGLE FEATHER. I wanted one from a bird still living. A killed eagle would offer me none of what I hoped for. A bird killed in the name of human power is in truth a loss of power from the world, not an addition to it.

My first eagle feather, one light and innocent, was given to me by a traditional healer I'd gone to see when I was sick. He told me a story about feathers. When he was a child, his home had burned down. All that survived the fire were eagle feathers. They remained in the smoking ruins of their home, floating on top of black ash and water. The feather he gave me was one of those. I still keep it safe in a cedar box in my home.

Where I live is in a mountain canyon. It is not unusual to see golden eagles in the canyon, far above us. One morning, after all my years of praying for a feather, I dreamed I was inside a temple. It was a holy place. Other people were there, looking at the ornately decorated walls, the icons of gold, the dried and revered bodies of saints, but my attention turned toward the ceiling. It was pink and domed, engraved with gold designs of leaves and branches. "Look up," I said to the others. "Look up." Still dreaming, I spoke these words out loud, and the sound of my own voice woke me. Waking, I obeyed my own words and looked up, seeing out the open window of my room. Just as I did, a large golden eagle flew toward the window, so close that I could see its dark eyes looking in at me for a moment before it lifted, caught a current of air, and flew over the roof of the house. I jumped up and ran barefoot outside to see where it was going.

If I told you the eagle was not in sight, and that there was a feather in the road when I reached it, you would probably not believe me. I, too, have seen how long it takes feathers to land, carried as they are by unseen currents of air. Once I waited for a hawk feather to fall. I covered distance, looking up, to follow it, but it never set down. It merely drifted until it was no longer in sight. But on the day of my dream, a feather was there. On the ground had fallen the gift of an eagle, soft white with a darker, rounded tip.

I know there is a physics to this, a natural law about lightness and air. This event rubs the wrong way against logic. How do I explain the feather, the bird at my window, my own voice waking me, as if another person lived in me, wiser and more alert? I can only think there is another force at work, deeper than physics and what we know of wind, something that comes from a world where lightning and thunder, sun and rain clouds live. Nor can I say why it is so many of us have forgotten the mystery of nature and spirit, while for tens of thousands of years such things have happened and been spoken of by our elders and our ancestors.

When my granddaughter, Vivian, entered her life in the world of air, I was at her emergence to greet her and to cut her cord, the sustaining link between her and her mother, her origins. When the bronze-colored stem of the baby dried, we placed it in a tall black pot until I could make and bead an umbilical bag to contain that first point of connection to this life, to keep her with us, safe and well.

One day a few months later, my parents visited. As always my father's presence turned us toward our identity and origins, so we brought out the cradleboard. My daughter, Tanya, dressed in her traditional beadwork clothing. Then, suddenly, with a look of horror, she said, "It's gone!" and ran toward the black jar that contained the baby's cord. She was right, the cord, the most valuable thing in our home, was no longer there. Because of the height and shape of the pot, and because of its placement on the shelves, it was not possible that wind might have carried it away. Nor could an animal have reached inside.

All that evening I searched, on hands and knees, under chairs, in corners and drawers, looking through the entire house, under furniture, on shelves, until no place was left unseen.

Several times throughout the night of searching, I opened a cedar box that contained tobacco, cornmeal, sage, and my first eagle feather, the one that lived through the fire. Again and again I returned to the box, puzzled by my own behavior.

Each time, as I opened it, I wondered why I was so compelled, so drawn to the container. It is a small box, with no hidden place where the birth cord might have been unnoticed, yet I returned to it. Opening it, looking inside, closing it.

In the middle of all this searching, a Blackfeet friend called to invite us to an encampment in Montana. "I'm so glad you called," I said to him. "I've lost my granddaughter's umbilical cord." I told him how terrible I felt about losing it and that perhaps the cord wanted to be elsewhere, maybe on the South Dakota reservation of my daughter's origins. Or that it was a sign to me that I have neglected my spiritual life, which I often do when working and living and teaching in a world of different knowings.

He told me a ceremony that might work. I hung up the phone and went to prepare the rite. Soon I was walking uphill in the dark moonlit night toward a cluster of trees where I made the offering. Around me was the song of insects, a nighthawk with its high-pitched call and clattering wings.

When I returned, I went once again to the cedar box. This time the feather, something else of value to me, was gone. I didn't know how this could be. Yes, I opened the box several times, but the feather never moved.

Getting down on hands and knees I looked under a chair, and I saw the eagle feather there, and the feather was pointing at the umbilical cord, so mysteriously now on the floor I had already searched.

It was the feather that took me to the baby's umbilical cord. The feather, that element of bird, so formed, so groomed to catch the wind and lift, that one-time part of a whole flying. It had once seen distances, had risen and fallen beneath the sun.

Perhaps there are events and things that work as a doorway into the mythical world, the world of first people, all the way back to the creation of the universe and the small quickenings of earth, the first stirrings of human beings at the beginning of time. Our elders believe this to be so, that it is possible to wind a way backward to the start of things, and in so doing find a form of sacred reason, different from ordinary reason, that is linked to forces of nature. In this kind of mind, like in the feather, is the power of sky and thunder and sun, and many have had alliances and partnerships with it, a way of thought older than measured time, less primitive than the rational present. Others have tried for centuries to understand the world by science and intellect but have not yet done so, not yet understood animals, finite earth, or even their own minds and behavior. The more they seek to learn the world, the closer they come to the spiritual, the magical origins of creation.

There is a still place, a gap between worlds, spoken by the tribal knowings of thousands of years. In it are silent flyings that stand aside from human struggles and the designs of our own makings. At times, when we are silent enough, still enough, we take a step into such mystery, the place of spirit, and mystery, we must remember, by its very nature does not wish to be known.

There is something alive in a feather. The power of it is perhaps in its dream of sky, currents of air, and the silence of its creation. It knows the insides of clouds. It carries our needs and desires, the stories of our brokenness. It rises and falls down elemental space, one part of the elaborate world of life where fish swim against gravity, where eels turn silver as moon to breed.

How did the feather arrive at the edge of the dirt road where I live? How did it fall across and through currents of air? How did the feathers survive fire? This I will never know. Nor will I know what voice spoke through my sleep. I know only that there are simple powers, strange and real. ☙

A Question of Style

Rachel Naomi Remen, M.D.

NOT ONLY CAN WE WITNESS MYSTERY; IN SOME profound way we are Mystery. Our lives may not be bounded by our history and may go on for longer than we dare dream. If Life itself is not fully defined by science, perhaps we too may be more than science would have us believe.

When Ahiro came to see me, he was in the final stages of prostate cancer. He had come to prepare himself to die. He was Japanese, a beautiful man who had lived with integrity and a certain elegance. His life had been his family and his work. From the beginning, he had a clear agenda for our meetings and took charge of them. He told me that he wanted to invite those who had blessed his life to come to our sessions, one at a time, in order to thank them for all they had given him.

Such an agenda is not all that unusual at this time in someone's life, but some of those he planned to invite took me by surprise. I had thought that he would invite his wife, his children, and some close friends, but among these beloved people were several of his professional competitors. Listening to some of his stories about them, I would have even said his enemies. But he felt a deep respect for them and believed they had spurred him to a level of professional excellence he could not have achieved without them. He wanted to thank them, too.

And so we began. About halfway through this agenda, as we were discussing the meeting we had just had with one of his sons, Ahiro suddenly paused in mid-sentence and looked at me. "Rachel," he said, "I am an educated man. I must believe that death is the end. And you, as an educated woman, surely you believe that death is the end also. Don't you?" Caught unaware, I looked back at him. He was leaning toward me, smiling, but his eyes were very serious. For the first time I wondered if our meetings had a deeper agenda than I had realized.

"I used to think that death is the end," I answered slowly, "but now I simply do not know. Death seems to me to be the ultimate mystery that gives life its meaning and even its value. I do not know if death is the end."

He sat back in surprise. "Why, surely you do not believe in a heaven with little angels flying about?" He looked at me and raised an elegant eyebrow. "Do you?"

"I don't know," I told him. There was a pause. Something shifted in his eyes, and I had the distinct sense that we had engaged each other on some level I could barely appreciate. Then he smiled at me and let the matter drop.

We continued to meet week by week with those on his list. But now in every one of our sessions, he would raise this topic, often when I least expected it, as if by catching me unaware, he might find out what I really believed about death. I shared stories and experiences. He shared from his extensive reading. I began to look forward to these discussions. They were wide-ranging and very animated, quite often funny and sometimes profound. Each time, after listening to his carefully reasoned arguments in support of the finality of death, I would tell him, "I still don't know." I think he found it frustrating. And intriguing.

During our next-to-last meeting, he again raised this issue. Hearing my "I don't know" once again, he began to laugh. "Rachel," he said, "I am an educated man. I *must* believe that death is the end. But just in case it isn't, I will come back as a great white crane and give you some sort of sign that I have lost this argument."

And then this tall and elegant man stood. Putting both hands behind him and folding one leg up, he tilted his head in an exquisite gesture so that for a heart-stopping moment he became a great white bird. We both laughed aloud in delight.

"Something about showing up as a great white crane is a little obvious," I told him. "Do you remember that duck on the Groucho Marx show that used to drop down on a string whenever a guest inadvertently said the mystery word?" "Yes," he said chuckling, "it's really not my style. I am more of a minimalist."

"Perhaps you'll find another way," I told him.

He looked at me for a considered moment. "I will do something that you will recognize," he said, suddenly serious.

Only a few months later, this remarkable man

died. Shortly afterward I was in the TransAmerica building, a large pyramid-shaped structure in the downtown business district of San Francisco, waiting for an elevator to take me to an appointment. The building is tall and so the elevators are quite slow. This gives everyone a few minutes to themselves. In this brief time, I found myself thinking of Ahiro and how much I missed being able to talk with him. I remembered some of the many extraordinary things I had discovered about him and what a delightful man he had been.

At last one of the elevators arrived. It was empty. And so with my heart and mind filled with memories of this relationship, I stepped in. The doors closed, and the elevator started upward so abruptly that I was thrown slightly off balance. I glanced down hurriedly to regain my footing and there, lying on the floor of the elevator, was a single, large, perfect white feather.

In my mind, I continue my discussions with Ahiro. As always, he has presented the issue in a way that I did not expect, and he has certainly raised the level of the dialogue. I still do not know if there is a life after death, but perhaps that is not really the point.

The important thing is that Mystery does happen and offers us the opportunity to wonder together and reclaim a sense of awe and aliveness. The feathers that fall into all our lives offer neither proof nor certainty. They are just reminders to stay awake and listen, because the mystery at the heart of life may speak to you at any time. ✐

Being a Feather

Mark Nepo

He sat quietly
as his father went silent.
Sometimes, his father
would look far off and
the shape of his eyes
would sag, and he knew
his father was carrying
the things that burn
where no one can speak.

It was then that the feather
appeared. He tried to guess
if it was hawk or crow or
maybe heron, but his father
said, "It doesn't matter
from which flying thing
it comes. What matters
is that it carries us back
and forth into the life above
and the life below."

His father held the feather
as if it were his own,
"It carries us into sky life
and ground life until
both are home."

His father placed the feather
in his hands. "Anything
that connects above and
below is such a feather.
The quiet is such a feather.
Pain is such a feather.
Friendship is such a feather.
The things that burn
where no one can speak
is such a feather. You
are such a feather."

Feather "Food" for Thought

Carole Louie

I HAVE COLLECTED FEATHERS SINCE MY daughter was a young child. When we were out on the beach together, she would bring a "feather gift" to Mommy. I knew intuitively that feathers were important, but not until I began to study metaphysics did I realize that feathers that catch your attention might be "harbingers" from the spirit world. Now, each time a feather appears, I hold it in my hand and listen for whatever message the feather is carrying.

One day, as I was taking something out of the freezer, I found a brilliant green feather stuck to the package. It was a natural green color, not dyed. I had never seen anything like it and I was shocked.

I held the feather and listened to it. It said that it would not speak to me directly yet and that I must ask for help.

Asking for help is not something I'm very good at doing, but my curiosity over what message this mysterious green feather could have for me overcame my reluctance.

That night I took the feather to my meditation group and shared the story with them. I passed the feather around, asking each person to hold it in her hands and see if any message came through for me.

As it turned out, everyone had some piece of the message to give me. One woman said she felt sure that the feather was an *apport*—a physical manifestation from the spirit world, transported by angelic forces. I tended to agree with her, since I had no other explanation for how it got into my freezer.

When I had received all of their messages, I knew that the feather had come to tell me that love was on the way, that a part of me had long been "frozen" inside, and that now it was time to "thaw out." By healing that frozen part of me, more love could come into my life.

I took the message to heart and focused on my own healing. Within a short time, I met a man who brought me more love than I could ever have received without preparing for it! Love was the teacher; the feather grabbed my attention so I could be ready to learn. ❧

Meditation

PLACES TO FIND FEATHERS

Go to a quiet place, indoors or out. Play some gentle, feathery music if you like. After a few moments of stillness, take out pen and paper. Make a list of places where you might find a feather (keep in mind that it's illegal to possess certain kinds of feathers—eagle, hawk, other raptors, and endangered species—unless you are of Native American ancestry or have written permission from the proper authorities). Compare your list to the following one, which lists where the feathers in these true stories were found:

* Along the highway
* Beside trash cans
* In backyards (front yards, too!)
* In campgrounds (even in your sleeping bag!)
* In dream catchers
* In dreams
* In elevators
* In flower beds
* In mailboxes
* In office buildings
* In open fields
* In parks or playgrounds
* In your refrigerator-freezer
* In vegetable beds
* In the woods
* In the zoo
* On beaches and along the shore
* On dirt roads
* On the hood of your car (look inside your car, too)
* On mountain hiking paths
* On the sidewalk
* On the street
* Under streetlights
* Under trees and bushes

Places where feathers can find you:
ANYWHERE!

We Will Dance Again

Janet Cunningham, Ph.D.

THE EXPERIENCE OF HAVING A FEATHER APPEAR *out of nowhere* as a symbol of encouragement from beyond is one that stretches my rational mind. Yet this experience happened in my presence and was witnessed by several people.

I was working as a hypnotherapist with a group of seven women who had similar memories of being together in a Native American past-life incarnation. Their past-life memories had surfaced through meditation, spontaneous recall, past-life therapy, bodywork, and art. Some of the women had memories of the total massacre of the tribe they had belonged to. They learned that the tribe's chief, Silver Eagle, had locked himself away in darkness: he had been tortured and forced to witness his mate and daughter as they were hung, drawn, and quartered.

On this winter evening, the women met in my office for a group regression in which they would attempt to unearth more of their lives from that incarnation and discern the purpose for their being together in this life. They arranged their chairs in a circle around the carpeted office space, and I gently took them back into their former lives as

Native Americans.

Just before the session ended, one of the women sensed the energy of the chief and channeled his message to the group:

> *You have accomplished here a very important purpose. While painful to relive, you have cleansed the soul of memories held tightly but best let go, as I have had to do. Some of the memories — the memory of the love, the sharing, the joyful times — can now be relived. Nourish that. Discard the bitterness, the hurt, and move on. I am very proud of my people. We will dance again. We will renew Mother Earth.*

A hushed silence filled the room. We had all sensed an extraordinary energy while the woman spoke. Finally, after continued discussion, the group began to prepare to leave. Suddenly one woman exclaimed, "Look! A feather." She pointed at the center of our circle. There on the carpet was a small gray feather.

"Who brought it?" I asked.

There were puzzled looks and silence. No one claimed to have brought the feather. The regression had taken place in an enclosed, windowless office space.

"Someone must have brought it or had it with them," I insisted.

The women continued to ask each other, "Is it yours?" but each woman replied that the feather did not belong to her. Finally the women began to move slowly toward the door, pondering this unusual appearance. Then, as if in response to our doubting minds, a second feather appeared on the floor in the center of the room!

We needed no further assurances. Somehow, we knew, Chief Silver Eagle had reached across time, space, and the unknown to give us this sign. It continues to be a sign for me of the close link between our "reality" and other unseen worlds. ✍

Native American Song

Anonymous

Screaming the night away
with his great wing feathers
swooping the darkness up;
I hear the Eagle bird
pulling the blanket back
off from the eastern sky.

The Eagle's Gift

Josie RavenWing

DURING THE TIME I LIVED IN ARIZONA, I SPENT countless hours wandering out in nature through the multicolored dunes of the Painted Desert and the mesas of *Dinetah* (Navajo land). It was on one of those walks that I found the beautiful raven's wing as an affirmation of the name I had taken.

Inspired by the wealth of wonders and places of power in the Arizona landscapes, I began to invite people from around the world to weeklong Desert Visions retreats. I took them to some of these power places, conducted ceremonies, and let the participants bathe in the subtle energies of the high desert country. Here they experienced healing, visions, miraculous moments of revelation and omens, and a deep appreciation of the power of Mother Earth.

Toward the end of a recent Desert Visions retreat, one crystal clear night, we sat by the fireside with a *Dineh* (Navajo) woman who has assisted me for many years and listened to her story. She is the granddaughter of a respected medicine woman who raised her and who is slowly preparing to leave this world, a fact that deeply saddens my friend. She recounted a series of events that had occurred in her life—a tumultuous and sometimes frightening period that was a full-fledged shamanic journey of her spirit.

At the end of her fascinating tale, she turned to me, her dark eyes glowing in the firelight, and stated that because of all that she'd gone through during that initiatory time, she was now "owed two eagles." She walked away into the night while I remained by the fire, trying to digest this statement and discern what it might mean. Finding no answers, I gazed into the star-studded skies, pondered the mysteries of the Spirit and my own equally intense shamanic initiations, and eventually wandered off to the comfort of my sleeping bag.

After the retreat ended, I began driving homeward, stopping here and there to enjoy some of the magnificent parks of the Southwest that I'd not yet visited. One of these places was Arches National Monument in Utah, a vast playground of ancient giants who had formed numerous massive rock arches in the course of their antics.

It was a hot, clear summer day. The sun squeezed glittering beads of sweat from my body as I hiked up the steep trail that led to Delicate Arch. Finally, after wondering how many more hours it would take, I rounded a corner and there it was!

Delicate Arch stands at the far edge of a huge natural stone amphitheater. Just past the arch the cliff drops straight down hundreds of feet, and snowcapped mountains whisper their secrets across the distance. I conquered my fear of heights and wound my way carefully around the edge of the amphitheater, past the multitudes of camera-slung tourists, and arrived at the center of Delicate Arch.

I stood there for some time, absorbing the evident power of this place, and then sat off to one side to contemplate the sheer, dramatic beauty of the view. My heart and spirit filled and I wanted nothing more than to stand and sing out my appreciation of this little corner of creation. I hesitated; there were so many people around that I couldn't quite get up the nerve.

But Spirit had other plans. Moments later, a raven came out of nowhere and flew so close that I heard the rustle of its feathers in the wind. It called out to me in no uncertain terms that I should go right ahead and sing one of the sacred songs that I knew from the Native traditions of this land. How could I deny my namesake?

I arose and walked into the center of the arch. I filled my lungs and then began to sing from my heart, my belly, my womb, my spirit. My voice echoed throughout the surrounding canyons, and my joy in being alive and present in this magnificent place exploded in a river of sound. All the experiences during the recent Desert Visions were there, too: the faces of the group glowing after their sweat lodge ceremony, their eyes filled with mystery after their vision quests, the coyote songs in the deep of night. All this and more filled me to overflowing and poured out of me as a celebration of the Spirit.

After I sang the song four times through — four being a number of balance and harmony — I moved from the center of Delicate Arch to the side again, noticing that the many tourists had become totally silent and still during my song. I took my bottle of drinking water, poured some of the clear liquid on the side of the arch as an offering, and spoke a quiet prayer that there might always be water for all people, creatures, and plants.

Within no more than thirty seconds of pouring the water, from what had just been clear blue skies, suddenly came tiny drops of cool rain! This light refreshing rain continued to fall on me as I hiked back down the mountain. When I arrived at my car it stopped, and I said thank you again for the blessing and the way it had made my walk so pleasant.

Soon I was on the highway heading homeward once again. The first brushstrokes of sunset were painting the rocks on either side of the road in warm red tones, and I basked in the colors and my love of this land as I drove along.

Suddenly my attention went to the side of the road where I caught a fleeting glimpse of something fluttering. Part of me knew immediately what I'd seen, and another part could not believe it. I pulled quickly to the shoulder of the highway and began backing toward the sighting. When I arrived, I opened the door of my car and, heart pounding wildly, approached what was around the other side of the car.

There it lay, its feathers fluttering in the late afternoon breeze. It was a young bald eagle, one that had recently finished its final flight. I immediately knew what had happened—saw the vision clearly in my mind. It had been hunting, and as it dove across the highway intent on its prey, it miscalculated, struck the edge of a passing truck, and fell to earth as its last breath passed from its body. It was young and not yet experienced in the ways of traffic. There it lay, power brought down from the heavens like the rain of only an hour earlier, resting at my feet.

I made a tobacco offering and brief blessing ceremony for the eagle's spirit journey. Then, knowing I simply could not leave its body to be mauled by passing vehicles or ravaged by the vultures that would inevitably arrive, I gathered it up in my arms. For the moment, it was a child that the heavens had given me to care for.

Once I had the eagle bundled safely in my backseat cooler, I began to drive and pray about what I should do with it. The eagle's spirit was a tangible presence behind me. I sang to it and praised its hunting spirit and its strength, alternately weeping and entranced by its power.

It became clear to me what must be done. I saw her dark eyes glowing by the fire and heard her voice telling me she was owed two eagles. I returned to Navajo land and delivered the first of the two eagles owed as a gift to the granddaughter of a medicine woman, to her grandmother for all she'd passed on to her, and to the *Dineh*, the People.

A Feather
with a Heart

Rev. Fern Moreland

WHEN I STUDIED FOR MEDIUMSHIP AND THE ministry, one of the first words I learned was the word *apport*. What does this strange word mean? It means, simply, moving an object from one place to another by a visible or invisible means. Some magicians do it by trickery, but my experience with apport came from the Spirit kingdom.

I was leaving my bank, located in the busy downtown heart of the city, when something made me look up. I was stopped in my tracks as I saw a little white object coming down out of the sky toward me. I looked up past ten-story buildings as it floated down and down, finally landing directly at my feet. I reached down and picked it up and was surprised to see that it was a sea tern's feather.

Others around me were looking up, wondering what kind of bird was flying, but nothing was in sight—only this one feather. I knew it wasn't a pigeon feather because of its shape. "Sea tern" kept coming through my mind. Granted, the Missouri River lay just north of the city, but I have never seen or heard of a sea tern being anywhere near. Where did the feather come from?

I pondered these questions as I drove home

and in the days that followed as I showed the feather to others. They hadn't seen a feather like it, either. I finally placed the feather in an Indian headdress I keep in my car.

Later, I attended a meeting of the Psychic Research Society. After the meeting, a man walked up to my car, pointed to the feather, and asked where I had gotten it. I related my experience. He looked at me skeptically. When I asked who he was, he gave me his name and told me he was an ornithologist.

"This is a sea tern feather that could only have come from the Great Salt Lakes region," he said.

"Really?" I replied.

"Really," he repeated.

Now it was my turn to be skeptical. But the feather was real, pure white, and beautiful. Who sent it to me? The answer became apparent a short time later when for the first time a spirit guide spoke to me, in a deep male voice, and identified himself as a prophetic voice. I called him Great White Feather.

The first time I heard the voice in my head, I thought, "Boy, Fern, you have lost your marbles."

"No, Fern, you are not insane," the voice reassured me.

Since that time I have heard Great White Feather's voice many times and recognize that voice as a conduit for God, or All in All, or whatever term you are comfortable with.

Great White Feather is not without a sense of

humor. One example of his antics happened when I returned a book to the library. At that time, I had a Toyota van and used the seat behind me for maps, an umbrella, and anything else I needed. I went to the library, deposited my book on the counter, and returned to the van. As I approached it, I noticed that everything that had been on the seat was knocked to the floor.

Who could have done this? I always locked my van and today was no exception. One by one I checked the doors, and all were still locked. Grumbling and puzzled, I unlocked the door and put everything back on the seat neatly. When I was finishing, something attracted my attention to the section between the two front seats, and there lay a feather, later identified to me as a quail feather.

The colors of the feather were some of my favorite: red, rust, brown, black. At its tip was the shape of a heart. I started crying. One of Great White Feather's signs to me was the apportism of hearts in many ways: heart-shaped buttons, heart-shaped feathers, heart-shaped pins, heart-shaped leaves dropped on the ground in front of me.

When we stay tuned to the Spirit, we progress more rapidly. I do not doubt that I speak to God and God speaks to me through feathers and through my spirit guide. Is God not the indwelling spirit in all living things? Whenever a feather is sent my way, it is God saying, "Fern, take heart. Everything is okay." ❧

Ask and You Shall Receive

Victoria Rose Impallomeni

Birds of a feather will gather together.
—Robert Burton, *The Anatomy of Melancholy*

I AM A NATIVE OF KEY WEST. FOR THE PAST twenty-five years, I have chosen a life of teaching marine environmental science to people who want to learn more about our link with nature by being *in* nature. I captain a twenty-five-foot "open fisherman" charter boat and take people out into the mangroves—God's jungle gym—to see birds, fish, and other wildlife at play in their natural habitat. This area is home to dozens of species of heron, tern, osprey, pelican, hawks, and cormorants.

We've come a long way from the days of my childhood when it was legal to shoot any and all birds, and my father used to shoot cormorants for target practice. Thanks to laws that protect these islands and coral reefs from the constant noise, diesel fumes, and oil slicks of speedboats and Jet Skis, this area can be a peaceful refuge for all sorts of rarely seen species.

When I open myself to connect with nature, amazing things can happen. I feel a special connection to birds, and my commitment is to teach people about how humanity has affected them. I have fought for laws to protect them. My spiritual name is White Heron Woman. I've often asked for—and received—feather gifts from my winged friends, but on this particular day I felt especially gifted by what happened.

Two Catholic nuns had scheduled a tour with me. They were longtime nature lovers, excited to have a day on the water, seeing close at hand what they had only seen in books. I wondered what they would think of my spiritual beliefs, which were more attuned to the *divas* of earth and nature than to any formal religion.

After we left port I took them to the first stop, a small island rookery that is a roosting island for the magnificent frigate birds that frequent the area. The name for these birds comes from the fact that they sail like the old frigate schooners. You may see them up high, riding the thermals, but you don't see them perched that often. They would be dead if they were in the water, because they have to have wind under their wings to take off. Frigates soar into flight, so they have to be up in the air to begin with.

We approached the island. It was the height of the mating season. I took the boat above the current and upwind, then turned the engine off so we could drift past the island in peace. I put on some beautiful music—Viennese waltzes, because these birds looked as though they were waltzing in the air.

The females, white-breasted with black heads, perched with their faces into the wind. The males, solid black except for red-pouched throats that inflated to attract the females, vied for positioning next to them. As the male frigates lifted off from their perches, they treated us to an intricate ballet. Their courting behavior was sensual and erotic, something you wouldn't see unless you were quiet and observed them for a while.

Entranced, we watched the whole scene until I saw that we were drifting too close to the island. Reluctantly, I started the engine to pull the boat away. The noise startled several frigates and they went into flight right over us.

I looked up and said, " If any of you have any extra feathers you don't need, could I please have one?" One frigate reached down, pulled out a large black feather, and dropped it. We watched, mouths agape, as the feather twirled in the wind and dropped toward the boat. The nuns gasped in wonder.

I silently thanked the frigate for his gift. It felt like real magic was happening here. I wondered how the nuns would interpret it. It didn't take me long to find out.

"It was as if the Creator got your message through to him," one of them said. The other one nodded in agreement.

That sounded close enough to me. ✍

Ritual

MANIFESTING FEATHERS

Find a quiet place where you can focus and concentrate. If you have a feather, hold it lightly in your hand. If you can be outdoors, climb to a hilltop or partway up the side of a mountain. Bring your feather with you.

* In meditation, ask for guidance on what you need to know at this point in your life. What quality do you need more of? What could help you on your spiritual path?
* Read the list of feather colors and their meanings on page 129. See if what has come to you in your meditation matches any of the qualities listed.
* Again in meditation, create the intention that a feather will come to you in some form as affirmation of the gift you have asked for. Picture yourself holding a feather of that color, your entire being bathed in the glow of the color you are holding.
* When your meditation ends, give thanks for any blessings you receive, including the blessing of all feathers that come to you in any form (pictures of feathers, birds flying, etc.).

In the days that follow, be aware of the presence or absence of the quality you asked for, and the color that is its symbol. Each time, renew your intention for a feather.

When your feather comes, don't forget to give thanks!

A Special Gift

Penny Wigglesworth

WE'VE HEARD IT SAID MANY TIMES THAT people come into our lives for a reason. We've also heard that there are *no coincidences*. Both of these statements have been true for me, especially since I met Seth Bailey.

As his hospice volunteer, I met Seth when he was sixteen years old. He was diagnosed with leukemia when he was three and underwent a bone marrow transplant at age seven. As a result of the radiation and chemotherapy, he developed serious kidney and lung problems. His mother took him to the world-renowned Children's Hospital in Pittsburgh, hoping he would qualify for a double-lung transplant. Seth's doctors told him that if he gained at least fifteen pounds, he would be a candidate for a transplant.

This was not going to be an easy feat; his disease had left him weighing far less than "normal" for his age. Back at his hospice home, he felt depressed and isolated.

We talked about hopes and dreams. I shared my dream with him about starting a little company in my home and running workshops where teddy bears (called "Penny Bears") would go out into the world of the seriously ill, sharing messages of love, compassion, and hope.

Seth really loved this idea and put his whole heart and soul into helping me develop our non-profit all-volunteer company. He helped us with the computer and had an idea a minute. He came to the workshops three times a week, where we knitted caps and sweaters for the bears and tucked shiny new pennies with the message "In God We Trust" into their special rainbow pockets. Our goal was to find homes for the bears in children's hospital wards, cancer units, and hospice locations throughout the nation.

Seth was no longer isolated or depressed. He had found new meaning for his life. He had found a purpose for living and began to gain weight. We made him vice president of our newly formed company, and soon he was put on the lung transplant list. We all had new hope for his recovery.

Shortly after he celebrated his seventeenth birthday, however, Seth grew weaker and weaker. He was admitted to the hospital. My beautiful, courageous friend left this life, gently cradled in his mother's arms.

She called to tell me the sad news. As I left my home that morning, I looked down and saw the most beautiful feather lying directly in my path. I had never seen a feather of this type before, and in that moment I *knew* that it was a gift from Seth. The tears flowed as I gently picked it up, knowing that I would keep it forever to remind me of this precious little soul whom I had come to love so much.

The next day, his mother came to my home.

We wandered out in my backyard, sharing stories of Seth and the wonderful contribution he made in the last months of his life. I told her about finding the feather. As we continued walking, we looked down and saw, right in our path, another feather— just like the one I had found the day before, only smaller. We looked at each other and smiled. Seth had given yet another gift, this time to her. I'd never seen this type of feather before, and I haven't seen one since.

Five years later, my feather is in the pocket of the very first Penny Bear. It reminds me of Seth and of his gifts of laughter, courage, love, and joy. He will always be in our hearts, guiding us and sending his love through every Penny Bear we send out. ✑

Follow the Feathers

Carolyn Elizabeth

IT HAD BEEN A DIFFICULT SPRING. I ESCAPED the floods and torrential rains in the Midwest and journeyed to Europe on a pilgrimage to see Mother Meera, a young Indian woman widely revered as the embodiment of the Divine Mother. I had planned this trip for more than two years with great anticipation and looked forward to receiving *darshan*, her special blessing of grace and light, bestowed on her followers through the power of her wordless gaze.

I stayed at a pension in Dornburg, Germany. It was a comfortable walking distance to Mother Meera's home in Thalheim. There, Mother received seekers from all over the world in the evenings; we shared in silence the awe of her enlightened presence. During the day, I had an abundance of free time to explore surrounding villages and the clusters of forests nestled between them.

During the first week I became familiar with the paths that led through the trees behind Dornburg. I was amazed at how inviting and accessible nature is in this part of Germany.

On the walk to Mother Meera's, I noted the thick cluster of trees between Dornburg and Thalheim and recognized the forest I had read about in Andrew Harvey's book, *Hidden Journey*. I knew Mother enjoyed meditative walks through the forest, and I considered these woods her personal sanctuary. This forest was holy ground I felt called to enter.

Here, I soon discovered, the paths were not clearly marked like the other forests I had spent time in. Exploring the woods like uncharted territory, I wandered through the lush green space and enjoyed the silence and solitude of this beautiful sanctuary for hours, losing track of both time and direction.

Finally, I realized it was time to start back or I would miss *darshan*. I looked around and could not find the path I had taken. Concerned, I walked in one direction, only to find a dead end. I went another way, and another, to no avail.

I panicked!

My concern quickly turned into an irrational fear: I would be lost in the dark forever. I didn't know which way to go. Finally, I stopped my searching and rested on a fallen tree. Tears streamed down my face. I felt cold, frightened, and alone. I did not know what to do. I closed my eyes and prayed for help.

Soon, I felt warm sunlight on my body. The atmosphere was otherworldly, and a mystical nature revealed itself. The light gently filtered through the trees and a powerful sense of hope filled me. I looked down and discovered a feather at my feet. Picking it up, I felt guided to walk.

The light directed me as feathers continued to

appear on the ground to encourage my way. Every time I came to a fork in the path, a feather appeared to beckon me toward the right choice. What was a terrifying experience became a playful exploration. I felt like Hansel and Gretel finding their way home.

One by one, seven feathers led me out of the darkening forest. Each was beautiful and unique, pointing the way unmistakably. At *darshan* that night, I knew I had already received the grace of God in the midst of the trees.

I returned home with those seven beautiful feathers. They continue to remind me of the Presence that is and the offerings that can be found if I am open to receive. ✑

My Name Was Golden Winged Hawk

Orazio J. Salati

AS FAR BACK AS I CAN REMEMBER, I'VE HAD an affinity for feathers and an affinity for things Native American, even though I was born in Italy. When my childhood friends and I played the American game of "cowboys and Indians," I always chose to be an Indian—even though I got "shot dead" by the cowboys.

After I came to America my fascination with feathers grew. Whenever I saw feathers I picked them up, noticing their deep colors, their unique composition. When I began painting, I liked to find feathers that were old and damaged. To me, they were more interesting if they weren't perfect. I've even painted with parts of feathers and included feathers in some of my mixed media paintings.

One day a friend who had been walking in the woods came across part of a hawk's wing and presented it to me. Again I felt a strange stirring, as if I had a greater connection to the hawk in some way.

Eventually I discovered why I had those feelings. Through hypnotic regression, I remembered being part of a massacred tribe of Native

Americans. The name given to me in that lifetime was Golden Winged Hawk. The hawk was a spiritual bird for me, and in our tribe we used hawk feathers for ornamental as well as spiritual purposes.

As an artist in this lifetime, somewhere in each canvas I paint is the image of a feather. It is as important to me as my signature. It is my link with Golden Winged Hawk—my personal reminder that feathers are not only things of beauty but have power to speak through time, through space, and through the gifts of others. &

Soul Feather

Jeanne Scoville

I GREW UP ON A BEAUTIFUL FARM IN WESTERN Wisconsin. My parents had a profound influence on me regarding the sacredness of nature. My mother often took us to the woods to pick berries or to gather walnuts and hickory nuts. I learned to ride horses at an early age and was at home in the woods by myself. I was particularly sensitive to wild creatures. They felt like family. As I look back now, I realize we shared a form of natural telepathy that remains with me to this day. It has been a deep wellspring of reassurance when I need to center myself amidst the modern haste.

As an adult, one of the places that allows me to center myself in the natural world is Wyoming. I make pilgrimages there as often as I can. One year, I felt powerfully inspired to visit Devils Tower, a sacred Native American butte in northeastern Wyoming.

My companion and I approached the tower in a state of reverence, just as we would enter a cathedral or other holy place. I asked for a blessing of the spirits before setting foot on the path surrounding Devils Tower and began my reflective journey.

As I circled the butte, I heard a rustle in the brush nearby. Investigating the sound, I crept close to a clearing where I came upon a large

Swainson's hawk in the act of killing a rabbit. I immediately "heard" from the hawk the message, "You may enter if you do not judge."

In my heart I silently acquiesced and continued to walk closer. I heard, "Continue in for thirty feet," then, "another ten feet" until I was about fifteen feet from the hawk and the rabbit. The hawk stared directly into my eyes and I felt completely at one with it and the rabbit. I understood that there was an agreement between them about what was happening. I went into a deep altered state and locked eyes with the hawk for what felt like an eternity.

I felt the profound and majestic power of the hawk wash through me. Then I heard, "You must go now. As you get near the path, I have a gift for you."

I respectfully turned and walked back toward the well-traveled path. As I reached the end of the clearing, I looked down and found three of the hawk's feathers lying at my feet.

"These are my gifts to you," I heard. "Give one to the ancestor spirits of this place, one to your companion, and one to yourself. Go now!"

I honored this request and spent the rest of the day in quiet, simple bliss.

My hawk feather now lies on my bedroom altar. It is a reminder of the blessings and teachings I received from my brother hawk. Its value is priceless; it is a most sacred treasure and a reminder of the Great Mystery of all of Creation. ✎

Riding the Feathers

Maril Crabtree

Feathers fall from wings

or from winged fingers

feathering thoughts

as they go

A Message from White Feather

Debra Hooper

SEVERAL YEARS AGO, SOME FRIENDS AND I attended a meeting to watch a psychic artist demonstrate her work, which involved drawing pictures of beings from the spirit world that she was able to "see" around her subjects. There were about sixty people present and Marie chose four or five with whom she wished to connect. I was one of the lucky ones chosen.

She had drawn a couple of pictures for others of relatives who had passed over when she looked at me and said, "You have a gentleman guide with you. He looks dark-skinned with long hair—he could be Chinese!"

She began to draw a sketch in pastel colors of the man she was describing, and after a few minutes, she handed it to me. I remember thinking, "He doesn't look very Chinese to me!" At that time, I was just beginning my spiritual journey and had no idea about guides or their purpose. I took the drawing home with me, put it in a drawer, and promptly forgot all about it.

Three years passed. I began sitting in a spiritual circle of friends. As we explored new understandings of our journeys, the subject of guides came up. I tried to connect with my spirit guide; although I could sense him around, I had trouble getting his name.

Over the months, a picture began to build, and I knew for certain that I had a Native American guide. I had seen him clearly, and so had several other members of the group, but whenever I asked for a name, nothing would come. It was very frustrating.

A year or so later, white feathers began to appear wherever I seemed to be. They would flutter down in front of the car when I was driving. They would be on the doorstep, in the garden, in the parking garage. I didn't know what to make of this onslaught of white feathers until one evening as I was meditating, the clear image of a blank, open book appeared in front of me and onto the page fluttered (you've got it!) a white feather.

To this day, I don't know why it suddenly clicked that evening, but I remember it dawning on me that this was the name of my guide. I announced this to the group, and they asked me to describe him. I was trying hard to do this when I suddenly remembered the picture. I went to the drawer where I had put it so long ago. Although the picture was done in oil pastels and had been shoved to the bottom of the drawer, it was still perfect in every way—not a smudge or crease in sight. I could not have asked for a better likeness of what I was trying to describe.

Confirmation of his name came later when we went to see another artist and her friend. The friend practiced automatic writing. She told me that there was a Native American with me and that he had a single white feather on his headband. She went into a deep meditative state and began writing. I still have the paper. It says, "I am White Feather. I love you."

Since then, I have had many conversations with White Feather. He is the person who looks after me; he works really hard with me. I also channel him from time to time, and he gives wonderful and sensitive teachings to us all.

Now, whenever a white feather flutters down by me, I just smile and say, "Hi there."

Meditation

ATTRACTING FEATHER ENERGY

Feathers can inspire your heart, brighten your home or workspace, and help you fly through the day. If you want more feather energy in your life, consider using feathers in these ways:

* *Apply* feng shui *principles.* If a relationship needs new wings, place a feather bouquet in that area; or place feathers in your work area if your career needs a boost. Feather energy can be used in any area where you want to create new beginnings, or movement where there is stagnation.

* *Use feathers to create a focus.* Select seven feathers, one for each day of the week, and keep them on your altar or in another place with spiritual energy. In a meditative state, hold each feather and let it "tell" you what quality it represents for you: love, courage, empowerment, compassion, freedom, surrender, and so on. Each morning, select the feather with the quality you most want to focus on for that day (or let it choose you), and keep it with you for the day. Like the bell that is rung periodically throughout the day at Buddhist monasteries and retreat centers to remind the listener to return to the present moment, a glance at the feather serves as a reminder to return to the focus for the day.

* *Create a feather mobile.* Feathers can remind you of a beloved memory, or they can be a connection to a favorite site. If you find several feathers in a vacation spot or other special place, create a simple mobile with lightweight dowel rods and nylon fishing line or thread. Hang it where a gentle breeze can keep the feathers in motion or by a doorway where the movement of people coming and going will be enough to start the feathers twirling.

- *Use feathers as gifts.* Include them in cards or letters; tuck them into raffia bows or other natural gift-wrap; lay one on top of another boxed gift, so that when the lid is lifted the feather is the first thing the recipient sees. If you're giving a book as a gift, a feather can be an added gift of a special bookmark. Carry a feather with you as an impromptu gift for someone you meet that day who could use a little extra feather energy.

- *Stay alert to other feather possibilities.* One woman had the image of a feather printed on her business cards because she wanted something that would stand out as a positive image in people's minds. "Invariably," she says, "people ask about the feather. I don't have one standard response—I rely on my intuition to tell me what each person needs to hear about that feather. Often it shifts the conversation to a deeper level."

Song of the Feather

Kenneth Ray Stubbs, Ph.D.

AT A NATIVE AMERICAN SUN DANCE, THE drum is always a major part of any dancing. Several people play the drum, chanting together as they drum the rhythm for the ancient songs. The drum is a catalyst for the dance, giving the dancers a beat, giving them energy to lift their legs higher, to become one with the deer, the buffalo, the eagle.

At a recent Sun Dance, I watched the dancing go on and on, song after song, chant after chant, the drum's cadenced beat bringing me into a near-trance state. Suddenly, the drum was silent. I found myself listening to the wind instead of the drumbeat.

In that silence, I saw a feather tied to one of the poles, twisting, fluttering, dancing in the wind. I listened to the feather's beat—so quiet compared to the drum but nevertheless carrying its powerful message, carrying the energies, singing the song of the wind. My mind flashed back to the times I saw hawks suspended among the clouds, far above, completely still except for the animation of a few feathers dancing in the wind.

At that mystical moment, seeing the lone feather fluttering from the pole, I could feel the voice of the wind speaking with the voice of the feather. I sensed the immense and unfailing power of all the ancient spirits of the elders merging with the silence and speaking through the feather.

In that moment I knew why I had apprenticed myself to a Cherokee shaman to learn how to align with the "sweet medicine" of his teachings. Their vast power transcends the ages, just as the feather and the wind speak an ageless message to anyone who listens for it. 🪶

Learning from the Crows

Greg Eric "Skip" Hultman

If men had wings and bore black feathers, few of them would be clever enough to be crows.
— Rev. Henry Beecher Ward

THERE IT WAS, A GLOSSY BLACK-BROWN-PURPLE iridescent flight feather nearly ten inches long, lying at the entrance of our driveway.

Although I was nearly a teenager, I was still a boy at heart. I picked up such treasures as bird feathers to keep for an imagined feather collection but with no real purpose. That morning was no exception. I ran to the back of our turn-of-the-century frame bungalow and ducked into our dim, musty basement. Clutching the feather and groping for a pull-string, I switched on the light bulb in the coal bin. I found the large jar kept on a shelf, unscrewed the lid, and placed my newfound treasure with the colorful mix I had already collected: blue jay, cardinal, goldfinch, pheasant, and others.

Finding the crow feather that morning did not stand out as an odd occurrence. Continuing to find a single crow feather in the same spot nearly every morning, right at the end of our sidewalk, did. I stopped saving crow feathers after the tenth or eleventh run to the basement. Yet they appeared regularly, all within the same area, usually at the end of the walk.

Not long after I started finding the feathers, the crows began awakening me. Every morning between 6:00 and 6:30, I would hear their raucous calls. Even during the cold winters, crows clung to their existence among the scrappy dandelions and renegade weeds of a school playground across from the house where we lived. The crows made their home in a half dozen catalpa trees that someone had thought to plant for the children's benefit many years before.

The lucky crows in the schoolyard made a good living. Besides the long, brown seed casings, which look something like dried-up foot-long hot dogs, the crows were able to find bits of food in the garbage left out for pickup. But somehow, those crows irritated me. Somewhere I had learned that they sometimes fed on chicks of less feral songbird species. As a young boy I lived in the suburbs and was forever exploring farm fields and prairies. I had grown to know meadowlarks, bluebirds, and other denizens of open spaces. In my mind, those birds had a higher pedigree than the lowly crow.

Now, however, I would hear the crows . . . only the crows . . . when I awoke each morning.

"Damn crows . . ." I spat out the words under my breath, fearing my mother would hear. I got out of bed and looked across at the schoolyard. There they were, black as coal, strutting, gliding, winging, roosting, fighting, and sometimes crying out in alarm.

I would ready myself for school. I would walk out the door . . . and there would be another feather. And each time I found it in almost invariably the same spot.

To make matters worse the birds acquired a new habit, as if to haunt me. After two years, I began attending the local high school. They started following me to school. The high school was slightly more than a mile away following a rather serpentine route complicated by numerous curved streets.

At first I didn't notice, but as the weeks passed, I realized that the crows were NOT the crows that lived down those streets I trod to school. These were the raucous feather-peddlers that had been waking me every morning.

When I returned to school in the fall of my sophomore year, the birds were there, following me as usual. It was then that I realized that they loved to grab an occasional grasshopper or other arthropodal morsel on the field I crossed next to their home school ground.

Eureka! That must be it. The *answer!* Smugly satisfied, I dismissed the matter of the feather leavings and the crows all together. The mystery was solved, I thought.

After Christmas break, I returned to school on a frigid Arctic morning when everything in Chicago was frozen so solid even the wind couldn't move. As I made my morning traverse, I realized that once again I had crow companions. Unsettling as it seemed, I realized that perhaps they were just victims of habit. As winter wore on, and food resources grew even thinner, I would see them less, I thought. January came and went, then February, and into March. The crows were indefatigable. They were still leaving their roost and following me all the way to school every morning.

I sought out my biology teacher, Mr. Getzmacher, and spoke of the mystery. He just laughed and said that it wasn't true. "What's a matter with you? Are you nuts or something?" It couldn't be they were following me, he said, and it was probably not even the same crows.

My self-confidence wavered. In those days, questioning a teacher about anything was unheard of, and if you did, it usually brought classroom retribution. So I let the official scientific inquiry cease.

I often made a game of keeping one or more of the birds in my sight, which was not so hard to do since the lack of foliage in winter meant I could see them move from tree to tree. One or two at a time would fly forward about a hundred feet, then stop. A couple more would come up to me from behind, as a rear guard. Sometimes they would stop to browse some hedge or lawn, or scold some daring grackle or starling that lingered too close. One time they stirred an owl from its sleepy roost. I think they were toying with it, knowing it as a mortal enemy of the night and aware that they had an upper hand in the daylight battle. It looked like aerial combat overhead, with the crows diving and careening in powerful, stunning moves.

Early each spring, my best friend and I made a ritual journey out to a small forest preserve on the edge of the city that was maintained by the county. We planned for weeks this early spring bicycle trip, taking binoculars to watch birds, packing lunches, bringing our simple black-and-white Brownie cameras. We even packed plaster-of-Paris to make casts of animal tracks. And when we traveled those eight miles, we finally got away from the crows of home, traveling too fast and too far for them.

When we arrived at those woods, we always ate our lunch first. We sat on a large rock in an open field, as the ground was always wet that time of year. Since it was the only rock around, it was the only dry place to sit. Then it would happen. The crows would come. They would make a game of dive-bombing us while we sat there, us munching, them scolding and laughing. Once we attempted snapping pictures of the winged marauders that seemed so close by, but when the film was processed, the photos showed only a black blurry spot against the undifferentiated gray of fields or sky.

My resentment grew as the ritual of crows following me continued, throughout my high school years. In the fall of my senior year, my beloved great-grandmother died. Great-Grandma Nora had been born in a sod hut in Nebraska in 1884. She had had a long, varied, and interesting life. She loved to tell family stories and had tried in vain to find someone interested in the family lineage. I had been the only one in the entire family who was. Consequently, she had shared many stories.

Her daughter, my grandmother, Grandma Fran, was now living with us, very ill with terminal cancer. Shortly after Great-Grandma's funeral, I was alone one morning with Grandma Fran, talking over breakfast. We began discussing the family lineage. I asked many questions, knowing that she would soon be gone, too. Among them, I asked her why Great-Grandma had always dodged questions of Native American heritage in our bloodline. She had always spoken respectfully of Native Americans to me, saying that on more than one occasion, they had literally rescued her and her family from starvation on the prairie. Knowing the family stories as I did, it seemed strange there were no Native Americans in our family's rather gritty American lineage.

Grandma Fran smiled a long, slow smile and in her melodious low voice, finally said, "But there was . . . " and she began the telling. I was astounded to learn that her father, my great-grandfather, was of the Pima Nation, and had been adopted and raised by whites. For some reason, he had blue eyes, so he could "pass."

I had never heard of the Pima. They were not the stuff of Hollywood movies, such as Sioux, Comanche, or Apache.

"Who were the Pima, Gram?" I asked.

She talked about a farming people, who raised cotton and beans and maize in the Southwest, where my great-grandfather had come from. The Pima had been a peaceful people but in spite of that had been mistreated by whites. She also spoke of a Cherokee grandmother "back East," and others in our family, further back.

I sat in stunned silence. I asked again, "Well, how come Great-Grandma never told me?"

She just chuckled and said, "Because I don't think she wanted you or anybody else to know."

I asked, "But why?"

She shrugged, "I'm not sure, fear I guess."

I was still too young to understand the hatred of "Indians" so prevalent among whites.

It was a moment in life when my personal landscape underwent a quantum shift, such as learning where babies come from, or that Santa Claus is really your dad. A lot of things became clear that morning: the headdress that was given to me as a child with an air of seriousness and pomp, complete with hand-painted eagle feathers; the incredibly flat feet I had. Growing up, I was badgered by strangers, raised near reservations, who said things like "Hey, are you sure you're not an Indian? You sure walk like one." Then there was the strange story of Grandma Fran's family being burned out of their new frame home on the farm in the Nebraska prairie by nightriders. There was an uncle who had fought in World War II on

Guadalcanal and was called "Injun Bill." All of it came back now—and so much fit together. My grandmother died a month later. We buried her on Christmas Eve. I cried deeply and long. She was a special spirit and I miss her to this day.

After that, the crows no longer left me feathers.

I was soon caught up in the whirlwind of life, with jobs, wives, and children. Although I never forgot about the crows, and the conversation with my grandmother, it was shuffled off to a corner of my mind. Not until many years later, after a serious illness, did I begin once again to reflect upon those crows.

Sitting one night in a cabin in the north Georgia mountains, I learned from a Native healer that the crows knew who I was before I knew myself. That's when I learned about the crows. Many Native American tribes believe the crow to be both wily and smart, which it is. A seeker of knowledge, a seriously intelligent animal, the crow flies into the Void and returns, always seeking answers to the Mysteries of Life and Death.

Those crows left a feather each day so that I would not forget the ancestors, Grandfathers and Grandmothers. Through the thin veneer of inter-marriage and assimilation, something stays different at the core of my being. I learned that Crow is and always has been a spirit guide for me. Because of this, I no longer fear the Void; it is another stop on my personal quest.

Today crows arrive in my life regularly, whenever they want to send me a message. Recently I came home from that trip to the mountains and the house sitter greeted my return. I had never discussed crows with this woman; I had never discussed my heritage with her. I had not mentioned a word of what had happened to me in Georgia—there had been no time.

Over breakfast she stepped out into the early spring cold and lined up a row of peanuts on the deck railing. Momentarily, a crow flew up and then another, and another. She came in grinning, explaining they had just started landing on the railing one morning a few weeks before. After a couple of days passed, she purchased some unsalted peanuts, and when they came again, she put out the peanuts. "Guess what I call them?"

I shrugged, not having a clue.

Beaming again, she said, matter-of-factly, "I call those "Skip's Crows!"

Stunned, I asked, "But why do you call them that?"

To which she replied, "Because they told me to . . ." and she slipped out the door on her way to work.

You Are Already on the Path

Kellie Jo Dunlap

SOMETIMES CHANGE IS HARD TO RECOGNIZE, even when—or perhaps especially when—it is right under our noses.

After years of becoming an accomplished bassoonist and playing in symphony orchestras, concert ensembles, and the like, I was frustrated. I enjoyed playing, but I was restless. I sensed that there was much more to life, and more for me to be learning and doing.

A friend invited me to attend a workshop on enhancing intuitive abilities through working with the energy field surrounding each body. It was an intriguing subject. I had already begun to experience flashes of intuition and insight amid the frustration. Sometimes "guidance" seemed to appear from nowhere. Recently I had "heard" a voice telling me that I should explore my artistic side and pay attention to my dreams. I had thought about making a dream catcher, which, according to Native American legend, captures and holds bad dreams while letting good dreams pass through. But the idea just sat there, stalled, as my whole life seemed to be.

At the workshop, the leader led us in a long

meditation, followed by a guided writing in which we were to ask questions we wanted answered and write down any answers that came. I asked the question that had become all consuming for me: What path should I now take for my life?

Immediately the "answer" came, and I dutifully wrote it down: "You are already on it." Nothing else—no great revelation, no specific answers. At the end of the meditation time, when the leader asked if anyone thought they did *not* get an answer to their question, I raised my hand and told him what I'd received.

"That sounds like an answer to me," he said, grinning.

"But I want a *real* answer," I complained. "Something definite and clear-cut. Like 'you should be an aerospace engineer,' you know." Everyone in the room laughed in agreement.

"Sometimes the universe only gives you one piece of information at a time," said our leader. "The important thing is that you acknowledge that this is, indeed, an answer, and a positive one, to your question of what to do next in life."

The next morning I was browsing the Internet, looking for feathers to purchase for the dream catcher I was making. I stumbled across a Web site called "Path of the Feather" and discovered a site outlining Native American teachings. I clicked on a button that said, "There are three steps to the Path of the Feather." When I clicked on the third step, the words "You are already on it" stood out, as if in giant red letters. I felt the hairs on my neck rise. Here were the exact words produced by my subconscious—or my guides—or whatever was responsible for having had me write them the night before.

As I read further, I understood that I was in the process of reinterpreting my life to include all aspects of me, and most especially the hitherto uninvestigated realms of the intuitive. I had only to continue to put one foot in front of the other to be "on the path" of my intuitive, spiritual self.

My spiritual path since then has been adventuresome. As with most of us who notice feathers, they seem to appear at appropriate times. When I made my own dream catcher, I used feathers I had collected over time. Each of them came to me at moments when I needed confirmation of life choices or just encouragement to keep up with the spiritual work I was doing.

Soon after I completed my own dream catcher, I dreamed I found a ton of duck feathers. In the dream I was told to put them on dream catchers. Shortly after this dream, I was driving on the highway behind an eighteen-wheeler that had an insignia resembling a dream catcher at first glance. The caption below the insignia read, "Cover the World." A closer look revealed some other picture, but—I "got the picture!"

I began making dream catchers for others. A friend bought more than a dozen to take back to relatives in Japan as gifts, so at least in a minor way I have helped "cover the world" with this wonderful visual reminder to pay attention to the stuff of our dreams.

What began as a tool for my spiritual path has expanded to include many others. In addition to making dream catchers and holding dream catcher workshops, I am deeply involved in healing work.

Feathers still come to me as reassurance that I'm on the right path, the most recent one being while I was again driving on the highway. A huge feather fell right in front of me out of the clear blue sky. I would have braked for it had I not been in shock and driving seventy miles an hour, still "jazzed" about a healing that had gone well the day before.

I am not the first to say this, but it seems clear to me that feathers connect us to the greater knowing that is in each of us. They connect us to Father Sky and Mother Earth. In our modern world, we have lost "in-sight," our connection to our intuitive self. A feather mysteriously appearing at a moment of illumination when we have actually made contact with this dormant self is a powerful reminder of the wisdom of that moment and the time long ago when we knew our connections to the environment and to each other.

Wings at My Feet

Starfeather

MY CONNECTION WITH FEATHERS BEGAN before I noticed. As a young adult, I spent many hours walking the beaches of Cape Cod picking them up, along with sticks and shells and stones. The gathering and walking were part of my emotional healing process. I had old spaghetti sauce jars full of feathers that I collected simply because I loved their beauty.

Slowly, I found my path to Spirit through meditation, yoga, beach walks, and a study of metaphysics. During one of my classes, we explored guided visualization as a way of receiving guidance. As I entered the meditation, I asked, "What is my life's work?" I had hoped to get a couple of clear sentences written on a chalkboard in my mind, but instead I got a movie. I saw a starry night sky with four white feathers coming to the center. These sparkling feathers were tied together with a golden cord. It was a powerful image rich with symbolism and it affirmed my path as a spiritual artist.

I believe that the purpose of "making art" or the creative process is for healing and that the finished piece is a reminder of that process. I saw the white feathers of my vision as a sacred paintbrush. Opening a small studio/gallery called Art & Soul, I created a workshop called Painting Inside Out, encouraging people (including myself) to express and heal their innermost selves. We painted in a free-flowing intuitive way, often using images we received from guided meditations. Some of my paintings had a Native American theme, and feathers showed up often in my work. The eagle feather, for example, is a classic symbol of connection to Spirit, for it has touched the clouds and fallen to the earth.

There aren't any eagles on Cape Cod, though. All around me artists were painting seagulls, sand dunes, and quaint scenes of Cape Cod Bay. I cared less and less about the commercial aspects of art and more and more about exploring this inner-art: meditation, automatic handwriting, and other psychic abilities. My focus was definitely changing. I began to wonder if I was doing the right thing, or was I losing touch with reality?

One day in my confusion I decided to turn it over to Creator. I went for a beach walk and said, "Hey, look! Am I on the right path or not? I need a sign, something that I will know for certain, something that affirms my beliefs." I walked farther, but I didn't see or feel anything that was in any way like a sign. On the edge of despair, I stopped again, and opened my arms to the sky. "This is *it* for me," I pleaded out loud. "Please show me that you hear me . . . that I am connecting. Or I must turn away from this path." My heart was raw with anguish, and I saw nothing. I felt no response.

Saddened, I looked down to take my first step

back home. There at my feet was a pair of seagull wings, one by each foot. This was my sign: wings at my feet! Suddenly, I felt truly seen and affirmed, as if Spirit had indeed written a big *YES* on my spiritual chalkboard with those seagull feathers. This sign gave me courage to continue on my path, relying on the universe to support my life choices.

A couple of years after my vision of the four white feathers coming together on the starry sky, I met the man I was to marry. A week after we met, he called me Starfeather as a sweet nickname. The hairs on the back of my neck stood on end: I had not told him about the vision. When he called me Starfeather, it felt as if he were speaking to my soul as the deliverer of my spiritual name.

The vision took on even more reality when a woman I hardly knew presented me with four sparkling white feathers. She said she was walking on an island path when she had a strong premonition that she was going to "find some feathers for Starfeather." Moments later in the path were the four white feathers, which she brought back to me. I have made a special beaded fan with them, which I use in my healing work.

Over and over again, feathers have been important signs for me. They are a way of receiving affirmation and acknowledgment that Spirit is not a figment of my imagination. Feathers are a physical manifestation of the Spirit that connects us all. They help me remember that anything is possible. ✎

Meditation

LIFE'S VISION FOR YOU

Raven Lamoreux-Dodd led this guided meditation for a group of twenty people. We listened to feather stories and then told our own. We sat in a circle, each with our feathers, and attuned ourselves to the universal powers that surrounded us. The room became charged with energy.

We ended the meditation with a spiral dance and the following chant while Raven drummed:

> We listen to the wind and dream
> > We stand in the wind and sing
> > > We fly on the wind
> > > > with our wings
> > > > > with our wings
> > > > > > with our wings

* Choose a feather of power or significant meaning to you.
* Standing quietly, close your eyes and grasp the feather lightly in both hands.
* Raising your arms, hold the feather to your crown chakra (energy opening in the center of your head). This is the connection with the divine. In your mind's eye, create a vortex of the color white and visualize it coming from the crown chakra. Ask the question, "What is the path for my highest good?" or say, "Please show me the path for my highest good."
* Move your feather to the third eye chakra (energy opening in the middle of your forehead) and create a vortex of the color purple. This is your connection with spiritual knowing. Again ask the question or repeat the statement.
* Move your feather to the throat chakra (energy opening at the base of your throat) and create a

vortex of the color blue. Ask the same question.

* Move your feather to the heart chakra (energy opening in the middle of your upper chest) and create a vortex of the color green. Ask the question again.

* Move your feather to the third chakra (energy opening in the solar plexus area) and repeat with the color yellow.

* Move your feather to the second chakra (energy opening about an inch and a half below your navel) and repeat with the color orange.

* Move your feather to the first chakra (energy opening in the area between your legs) and repeat with the color red.

* Finally, sweep your feather slowly back up your body, visualizing a rainbow of the colors you've created, until your arms are once more above your head. Move the feather above your head, stretching your arms skyward as high as possible. Repeat the question once more, and thank the universe in advance for the answer that will appear.

You can do this meditation whenever you need direction or confirmation that you are on your path. ✐

Part Two

The Power of Feathers:

Messages of Healing and

Transformation

Feathers and Dreams: An Interview with a Jungian Analyst

Maril Crabtree

FEATHERS THEMSELVES ARE CONCRETE, TANgible objects—part of a bird's wing, finely constructed to accomplish what nature dictated. Although color, size, and shape may vary, the basic components of a feather never change.

What feathers mean, however, is *not* tangible, although it is more or less definable, and the meaning may change from one circumstance to the next. What feathers mean can be as ephemeral and intangible as a dream.

But the world of dreams has its own structure, its own geography, its own set of symbols and meanings. Dream interpretation existed in biblical times and in the days of Greek oracles. In more contemporary times, the work of psychotherapists such as Sigmund Freud, Alfred Adler, Carl Jung, and Erich Fromm relied heavily on dreams as doorways to the hidden psyche, expressions of the unconscious, and valuable signposts of direction for our waking lives.

When I meet with Jungian psychotherapist Mary Dian Molton to discuss feathers and dreams, our conversation takes us into all these realms and more. We sip tea and eat slices of orange in a cozy home office surrounded by books, Oriental rugs, and a desk lined with papers. It is cold and snowy outside; the blank gray sky has erased all evidence of birds for the moment.

"If someone dreamed of a feather," she says, "I might associate it with Spirit. Feathers can be a symbol of that which carries us into the imaginal world, or the spiritual world. They can be a means of finding one's fantasies. They can be a sign of that which is, quite literally, created 'out of the blue' — out of the systems of the psyche whereby an idea is given a form, a symbol."

Mary Dian pauses and sips her tea. "There isn't anything in the world of form that didn't originate with fantasy. This chair, this cup, this pot of tea," she gestures, "none of it existed in physical form without first having existed in thought, in fantasy. If feathers represent that flight of fantasy, that connection with the realm of imagination, then you could say that there was once a feather for a cup, a feather for a pot, a feather for everything you see around us."

While I digest this along with an orange slice, she continues, "In the symbol is the transformation. There is the archetypal longing to fly, as in the myth of Icarus. The ancient Egyptians had a belief that, at the moment of death, the soul was weighed on a balance scale with a feather on the other side, the feather representing truth. The Aztecs revered

Quetzalcoatl, the feathered serpent, as a powerful symbol of fertility and life. So the feather, you see"—she smiles as she raises the cup to her lips again—"can represent transformation at both ends of the spectrum."

By now my head is swimming—or flying—dreamlike, in a state of feathered bliss. I think of the famed phoenix, the mythological Egyptian bird with a life span of 500 years, consumed by fire and rising from the ashes: the bird of death and resurrection that can be interpreted as a symbol of spiritual rebirth. I think of the gods and goddesses throughout the ages portrayed with feathers or wings, or as magical birds: Zeus transformed into a swan, angels dancing on the head of a pin, the feather-covered Papageno in the opera *The Magic Flute*. I feel the confusion that psychic dream analyst Edgar Cayce, who interpreted thousands of dreams in the first half of the twentieth century, referred to when he dreamed of "flying feathers."

When I mention his interpretation to Mary Dian, she nods in agreement. "Frequent dreams of flying might also mean that your spirituality is ungrounded, that your life is quite literally 'up in the air.'"

We talk about "The Three Feathers," the famed fairy tale of the Brothers Grimm, in which the old king, in order to choose his successor, set his three sons the task of bringing back the most beautiful carpet. To avoid any disputes among them, the king blew three feathers into the air and directed his sons each to follow one feather. The two "smart" brothers watched as one feather flew east, one flew west, and the third flew straight ahead, and then fell to earth. They quickly went right and left, mocking the "dumb" brother who had to remain with the third feather where it had fallen.

But this feather pointed the way down, literally, into an underground lair where the dumbling found the boon that won him the kingdom. In Mary Dian Molton's written analysis of the tale, she explains that what was needed would not be solved by logic or reason, but would be left in the hands of fate. "Such is the feather," she writes. "We can think of the wind that blows the feathers as the spirit . . . the spirit that moves things around in psyche, that understands the idea of 'the fullness of time, the part of psyche that is inarticulate, dumb, slow to grasp, farthest away from one's daily use. It is the magic solution."

Shades of Forrest Gump. Remember that little white feather that hovered around him, showing him the way? Or was it simply "fate" after all? I pose the question aloud.

"*Fate* is another term that's hard to define fully, and to me it seems far from simple," Mary Dian responds. "To the Jungian, fate could be thought of in many ways. One of them could be simply 'synchronicity at work.'"

I picture the great ageless hand of synchronicity, hovering over the dream-cauldron, stirring the soup of the psyche to see what archetypes are brewing. Feathers, wings, and flight are among the most ancient of symbols that stir our longing for connection to the powerful world of air, light, and spirit, our desire to "slip the surly bonds of earth" and transform ourselves into something perhaps unrecognizable except at the level of soul, or what the soul symbolizes.

In the symbol, after all, lies the transformation.

Spirit Feather

Denise Linn

DURING MY LIFE, I HAVE HAD THE OPPORTU-
nity to spend time in a number of earth-based cultures throughout the world. In some of these native
cultures I have been gifted with a name. This is an
honor and it connects me to the people of the tribe
or culture. To the Zulu, I am called Nogukini. To
the New Zealand Maoris, I am called Whetu-
Marama-Ote-Rangi. Thirty years ago when I
studied the ancient Hawaiian traditions with a
kahuna (shaman), I was given the Hawaiian name
Maileonahunalani.

I cherish the names I have been given through
the years; however, I had a desire to be given a
spiritual name that reflected my own Native
American culture. I prayed that this name be gifted
to me directly from the Creator.

One sultry summer afternoon, I felt an urge to
walk into the woods that spread for miles in the
Cascade mountains near our small mountain home.
I had wandered there often, always finding mystery
in the most ordinary things: the way the leaves cast
their lacy patterns across the path when the sun
was high overhead; the rustling sounds of creatures
making their homes all around me, yet invisible to
me most of the time; the abundance and almost endless variety of berry bushes, wildflowers, variations

of evergreens, all living together peacefully and cooperatively.

Climbing to the top of a pine-covered hill, I stopped under a large old tree and lazily closed my eyes. It was peaceful and quiet. There wasn't even the normal background chatter of birds or the hum of insects. I have rarely experienced such stillness. I sat for what seemed like hours, eyes closed, aware of the light breeze playing through my hair, waiting for Spirit's sign.

Suddenly, I sensed a change in the forest air. It felt as if subtle ripples of energy undulated through me. Taking a deep breath, I slowly opened my eyes. A few feet in front of me, on a branch, was a great horned owl. He was so close that if I had reached out I could have stroked his feathers. He didn't move but looked straight into my eyes. The woods seemed to fade away until all that was left were his enormous eyes. It seemed as if we were breathing our essence into each other. Then, with a blink of his eyes, the old owl lifted his massive wings and silently glided away into the forest.

After a few moments, the afternoon sounds of the forest returned, as though nothing unusual had happened. Slowly I rose and went to the branch where the owl had landed. Three small, white down feathers lay clustered there. I picked them up and held them, marveling at their soft texture and dazzling whiteness. Suddenly, I heard an inner voice saying, "Put the feathers in your medicine bag now." The words puzzled me. I had a beautiful deerskin medicine bag, but today it wasn't with me. Again I heard the voice. "You are your own medicine bag," the voice insisted. "Put the feathers in your medicine bag."

The invitation seemed clear. I was being asked to take the feathers into my body. Without further thought, I put the downy white feathers into my mouth and swallowed them. As I felt the feathers work their way slowly down the back of my throat, I could feel my spirit expand. The inner voice continued.

"Owl medicine goes with you. It is the medicine of seeing through the layers of darkness into the light. Just as you have taken owl feathers into your body, the spirit of Owl has penetrated your being and will always be available to you."

Gradually the vision faded and the voice died out. I came back to the reality of the woods surrounding me, with a feeling of lightness, openness, power, and strength that continues to nurture me to this day. And to this day I carry my Spirit Name of White Feather. ❧

Teachers in Dreamtime

Gina Ogden

The grandmothers came to me and said:
We are many.
Our hair is white as feathers
Our skin is soft and shiny as rocks.
We come in the mist.
We are the moon
We are the light
We are the eye in the paw of the puma
the prayer in the wing of the eagle.

Our hands are the fire in the earth
the rainbow in the rock.
Our medicine is strong.
We hold you like a suckling bird.
We feed you the glowing coals of truth.

Our song is the pulse of the drum
The roaring inside your heart.
Listen.
Our voices run like water over the rocks
all the way to the ocean.
We call forth the roaring
in every being that moves.
We are the breath of life

the wind in the wheat
the whisper in the ear.
On our tongues we hold the bread of knowing.

We are the grandmothers.
We are the stars
We are the moon
We are the mist
We are the standing stones.
We are silent as feathers.
We come suddenly in the night.
We shall not be moved.

From the Heart
of the Eagle

Maril Crabtree

DON ALBERTO TAXO LOOKS LIKE THE PIC-tures of Jesus some of us grew up with: slight in stature, olive-skinned, shoulder-length dark hair curling casually around his head like a natural halo. He dresses simply in white cotton shirts and pants, with sandals, the way many ordinary people of his native Ecuador dress. But the energy that emanates from his presence is far from ordinary.

I had heard that this man healed with feathers and wanted to see him in person. I had made arrangements to talk with him privately about his feather healings early in the afternoon, prior to his public talk, but his plane was delayed and he arrived only minutes before his scheduled appearance.

I hurried to the auditorium. Most of the seats in the large room were occupied and an anticipatory buzz filled the air. I stood at the back of the room as he came in. I was quite unprepared for the power I felt as he entered. I was even more unprepared for what happened when I was introduced to him.

His interpreter pointed me out and he came toward me, smiling. I stuck my hand out, but he took both my shoulders in his hands and embraced me. The force of something I would call "immense compassion" enveloped me and swept through me. Then he turned and started toward the front of the crowded room, leaving me feeling as refreshed as if I'd taken a leisurely walk through a garden of blooming flowers and exotic plants.

Don Alberto spoke to us that evening as the spiritual leader of eleven Latin American communities, appointed by the Shamanic Council of Iachags (healers, shamans, and seers) from the Ecuadorian Andes. Son and grandson of shamanic healers, he knew at an early age what his gifts were, although he never expected to be chosen as "The Force of Great Light" (the title bestowed on him by the Council), to be the bridge between North and South America for the sharing of ancient prophecies and healing knowledge.

His words to the gathered audience were simple: When the eagle of the North can fly with the condor of the South, the world will be transformed. Both eagles and condors are birds of great strength and wisdom, and together they represent the mind and heart of the world. There is much to learn from the union of the two, he said through his interpreter.

How strange, I thought, that this man, who cannot speak English, who grew up in poor native villages and still lives most of his life as a village healer, would be chosen to speak words of transformation to audiences of sophisticated Westerners.

I thought again of Jesus, of his birth in a manger and his humble village life, of signs of his early wisdom when at the age of twelve he took on his spiritual elders in much the same way that Don Alberto, at the age of fifteen, had challenged his shamanic elders to release their ancient secrets for the good of the entire planet.

"When the light from the heart of the eagle shines forth, it will illuminate the world," Don Alberto said. "The heart knows how to feel. Allow your heart to be connected with the elements of nature—the air, the water, the earth. When you *feel* the connection, you are close to the Creator." I thought of all the times I'd found feathers: always in nature, always bringing me a feeling of blessing from the invisible spirit world that I know exists, because in those moments of connection *I feel it*.

"Let each place and each moment be sacred," he continued. *"Simplemente sentir.* Simply let yourself feel."

He sang shamanic songs in his native language and invited us to join him by chanting or humming whatever sounds came to us at the same time. "Don't concentrate on the words," he said. "This is an invitation to the heart. Your heart will feel the words, and learn the rhythms."

For the next five minutes, we filled the room with beautiful sounds, inspired by the simplicity of his invitation. As each individual chanted from the heart, eyes closed, the sounds wove themselves together in efflorescent harmony, giving new meaning to the phrase *music of the spheres*. Then he took his bundle of feathers and invited our

Western spiritual leader to receive a healing "for the benefit of all." The minister came forward and Don Alberto directed the feathers to the energy aura surrounding his body. As Don Alberto brushed the feathers from the minister's head to his toes, he chanted softly in his native language.

The feathers ascended the minister's spine slowly, cleansing and purifying, and paused in front of his heart as Don Alberto chanted. He smoothed and brushed both sides of the minister's body as he worked and finally, in what was clearly a blessing, put the feathers on top of the minister's head.

The energy of condor and eagle—mind and heart—had been united and connected in the physical body, as well as in the spirit. At that moment, I felt peace settling within my own body, an ineffable sensation of inner well being. I recalled an old childhood hymn, "Standing in the Promises." Standing in the promised unity of heart and mind, I felt renewed and blessed by this global commitment to connection.

Ritual

HEALING WITH FEATHERS
Don Alberto Taxo

Don Alberto Taxo, through his translator, gave the following instructions for using feathers in a healing ritual. By using feathers, you are bringing the element of Air into your ceremony. By connecting with this element of nature, you invite connection and sensitivity to all of nature.

* Begin by asking the Wind to pass the energy from the feathers into the aura of the person asking to be healed.
* Use the energy of the feathers to remove negative energy from the body, brushing from right to left for this purpose, or brushing from left to right when you want to collect positive energy.
* By placing the feathers on different parts of the body, you can in this manner send away negative energy and restore positive energy.
* Use wide, tall feathers to help get rid of negative energy and short, narrow, more colorful feathers to bring positive energy into the body.
* As you gently brush the aura surrounding the body, ask the feathers to protect and purify the body with their energy, to bring harmony and balance to the aura.

The Power of the Eagle

Bobby Rae Sullivan

WHEN I WAS GROWING UP ON OUR RANCH IN southwest South Dakota, my mother often talked to me about the eagle and how important it was to our people, the Oglala Sioux. If you saw an eagle while you were traveling, for instance, the trip would be a good one. If the eagle dropped a feather while it was flying above you, it was the best medicine of all and you could use it to help yourself or others.

During my lifetime, my mother had three eagle feathers come to her. These three feathers she kept, telling me that it was meant that she use them for some special purpose at some time in her life. I never gave it much thought, but it was an awesome sight to see one of the feathers come floating down out of the sky right above our pasture, while the eagle was in flight. She found one of the other feathers close to where the eagles nested on a butte east of our home.

The last one came to her shortly after a friend died unexpectedly. We had just returned from the funeral and saw the feather lying in the road, right in front of the gate to our pasture.

"I'm sure this is a message from him," she said, smiling. "When he and I were kids and used to check cows together, every time he saw an eagle he would tell me that someday he would be soaring up there, looking down on everyone. He said that he would drop a feather on the people he cared for, and for those he didn't like he would drop something else!"

Many years passed. I married and gave my mother three grandchildren, all girls. My first daughter was healthy and agile. My second daughter had some problems but soon outgrew them. My last child, Lisa, came into the world healthy, but by the age of three developed seizures from an extremely high fever.

As the seizures continued year after year, I frantically took her to doctors to try to find out what could be done. Nothing seemed to help.

When Lisa was seven years old, my husband was preparing for a Sun Dance and I asked him to include Lisa in his prayers. My mother handed him the three eagle feathers she'd been keeping all these years.

"I feel like this is the reason I've kept these feathers," she said. "Please take them and use them while you're dancing and making your prayers for Lisa."

A short time later, my brother took me to a sweat. During the sweat, I told the medicine man that I was praying for my daughter, who was ill. After the ceremony was over, he took me aside and said, "Your daughter already has some powerful medicine working for her through the Sun Dance.

The power of the eagle is working for her and it is a strong power. By her eighth winter, your daughter will be free of this illness affecting her mind and body."

I was elated but shocked at his words. I had not told him anything regarding my mother and her eagle feathers, my husband, or the Sun Dance he had participated in on Lisa's behalf.

When my daughter celebrated her eighth birthday, she did it without the benefit of all the medications that she had been on. She had been seizure-free for about four months. I remembered all the stories my mother had told me about eagle medicine, and that the power of the eagle is strong when used in the right way.

My mother was not surprised by the news that Lisa was no longer having seizures. When she gave the feathers to my husband, she told me, she felt their power travel to him. ~

Beacons of the Night

Eleanor K. Sommer

OWLS HAVE ALWAYS CREPT INTO MY PSYCHE as symbols of mystery and wisdom. Even as a child, I loved to listen to the deep calls of the owls that populated the woods surrounding our New Jersey home. Every now and then I would see their wide eyes and massive wingspread, hear the swoop of air as they lifted from a branch in search of prey. Night hunters. Specters of death. Sharp-eyed visionaries. The owl sees what others cannot. The owl does not always bring happy news, but it is a powerful symbol of transformation.

My residency in the woods ended when I moved to Florida for college. My glimpses of owls came only on visits home, on camping trips, or when I visited friends who lived in less populated areas.

It wasn't until I moved to Naples, Florida, that owls once again became a regular part of my life. Two nearby towering pines were home to a pair of great horned owls, probably residents long before we moved in. Their familiar calls and ethereal presence rekindled my bond with these great birds of prey.

Our neighborhood had a small park in the middle of it. A live oak, a handful of palms, and some pine trees made perfect perches for owls and a nice vista for the residents. My husband and I often walked around the park at dusk, listening to owls as they prepared for their evening foraging.

The walks always relaxed us, especially as we wrangled with some tough decisions about moving to a different part of Florida. We loved Naples, but it was becoming crowded and commercial. We longed for "old Florida." Our walks became meditative discussions. Should we go? Should we stay? I posed the question one night out loud to the stars and opened my arms to the sky. At that moment, a moment that seemed like surrender, one of the owls swooped down so close to my head I felt its tail-wind brush my hair.

"Well, there's your answer," my husband exclaimed.

Indeed it was an answer. Transformation. A change. A sign that it was time for something new.

The next morning my insight was confirmed when my husband brought in an owl feather that had fallen on our driveway. "I think this is probably for you," he said.

Our avian friends were almost run off by the screech of buzz saws that claimed one of the trees in the stand of pines they called home. Our callous neighbor was frustrated with pine needles falling on her car. Move the driveway, I suggested, but down came the tree.

At our going-away party, a friend brought me an envelope of several owl feathers that she and her husband had found on a camping trip. I tied them together with my owl feather and some sea-worn rocks and shells from my favorite beach in

Naples: memories to carry with me inland.

Good-bye, owls. May your home be safe.

We rented space in a house in Gainesville, a north central Florida community known for its spectacular tree canopy and surrounding miles of undeveloped land.

We looked for land to buy. We drove and drove, got lost on dirt roads, were chased by dogs, and lied to by real estate agents. We settled on a piece of land and bought it before we had spent the night on it. When we finally camped, we were met by a glaring security light belonging to a neighbor. It illuminated our five acres like Disneyworld, creeping into the trees and casting bizarre shadows. The majestic live oaks that could have dimmed the unnatural pink glow reached too far west to allow room for the house. Worse than the lights was the silent morning sky.

"Do you hear that?" I asked my husband upon awakening.

"Hear what?"

"Exactly," I said. "No birds!"

A combination of the light, a nasty neighbor, and the dearth of wildlife put us on the road again.

We finally discovered acreage close to town and obtained permission to spend the night *first* — before signing any papers. This lovely forty-acre piece of property with a creek meandering through it was more than we could afford, but friends were interested in sharing the expenses in order to restore and preserve some of the land. It was also adjacent to several hundred acres of land already preserved by two communities with strict rules against tree-cutting and wayward development; we hoped for no surprises on our overnight visit.

As the sunset faded behind the pines and sweet gums, a breeze glided over the open field where we imagined our home. Birds and frogs and crickets actively took up the evening song. We were pleased. This land was alive!

When the gray blanket of night covered the trees, I heard a faint hoot, then a louder, *hoo, hoo-oo, hoo, hoo*.

I could feel my husband's smile through the darkness.

"You heard it?"

"I heard it."

More than a year later, we finally moved into our modest cabin, glad to be part of a community with a love of nature and rules against outdoor lights. Our owl friends were assured of good neighbors who desired to protect the habitat.

The next day, I ventured outside in the chill of the December morning. I inhaled the pine-scented air and watched my breath hang like smoke as I exhaled into the frost.

As I looked down, I saw, just inches in front of my toes, a feather. An owl feather. I felt transformed, alive, and ready for a new adventure in the woods.

We hear them often, screeching as they descend upon their dinner, hooting as they pass signals and declare territory. Beacons of the night. Seeing what we do not. Guiding us toward transformation. ✎

One Spirit, One Feather

Hazel Achor

MY SPIRITUAL JOURNEY WITH FEATHERS began many years ago in California. About fifteen of us met weekly to explore spiritual principles beyond what we had learned in our traditional faith upbringings. We called ourselves "The Omega Fellowship" and met in each other's homes. As our meetings continued over several years, we grew closer.

Then one of our members, Claude, had a heart attack. He and his wife, who could communicate on psychic levels with each other, agreed that if he died, he would send her a symbol of his continued presence. After three days on life support, both his wife and his best friend, who also had not left his side, saw his spirit leave. Life on the physical plane, at least, had ended for Claude.

Although I attended his memorial service, our first Omega Fellowship meeting without Claude felt incomplete. We struggled through our agenda, but finally I voiced what I suspect everyone had been feeling.

"I keep thinking about Claude," I said. "I miss him. I wish there were a way to have him still with us."

"He is with us," his wife, Delores, said, smiling through her tears. "Maybe if we all meditate together, he can join us from wherever he is."

We silently gathered in a circle and prayed for Claude's spirit. It felt comforting to be holding hands and focusing on our old friend, wishing him well. We stayed that way for a few minutes and then each of us prayed a few words aloud.

When everyone had finished, we opened our eyes and looked down. There in the center of our circle was a large feather, similar in size and markings to an eagle feather or large hawk feather. A look of wonder and pure joy flashed across Delores's face.

"That's the symbol we agreed on before he died—a feather!" she said. "All through our lives, wherever we traveled, we collected feathers. He said that his spirit would send me a feather to let me know he was all right."

No matter how skeptical I had sometimes been in my spiritual journey, that night I became a "believer" in the fact that our souls survive beyond this physical plane. Since that time, feathers have often appeared as a sign of support when I was going through a transition. But I'll never forget the feather that simply materialized. Whether it was sent by Claude's spirit or whether we drew it to us from somewhere in the universe, it remains a miracle of interconnectedness.

Feather Journey

Anna Belle Fore

MY PATH WITH FEATHERS BEGAN DURING A
meditation guided by Ernestine Cline, a psychic
artist from Fort Myers, Florida. As Ernestine
guided us on an inner journey, she told us to see
ourselves receiving a gift from a wise one. There
was no hesitation from my inner being; I saw my
gift clearly. It was a large black feather on a white
satin pillow.

The next day in my meditation at home, I was
given another black feather. A short time later, I
was given a white feather and then a red one. What
was the significance of these symbolic gifts? I wondered. Their meaning was a mystery to me. Of
course, I appreciated the beauty of feathers, but I
didn't know what to make of them appearing in my
meditations.

At this time, a dear friend and I took a trip to
California on a self-discovery excursion. At our first
stop, I stepped out of the car and there at my feet
was a single black feather. The next day as we
walked, a white feather appeared in my path. I
began to be aware of how often feathers came across
my path. By now, I was looking for a red feather!

In a small northern California resort community, we stopped in a Native American shop. I
looked everywhere for a red feather but saw none.

As we were leaving, I asked the shopkeeper if she had any other feathers. She disappeared into the back of the shop and came back with a small bag of red feathers. These feathers had been at the shop for a while, she said, but for some reason she had not put them out for sale. Of course, I felt that they were just waiting for me! These feathers confirmed that my recent decision to pursue healing as a vocation was the right one.

I now frequently find feathers. They make me smile and laugh. I even found a white feather in the bathroom where I work. Until then, I was a little disgruntled that my job as manager/administrator of a healing center included emptying the bathroom trash each day. Finding that feather was a message to "lighten up" and see beauty in everything.

Each time I see a feather, I know it is a beacon showing me that I am on the right path. ✍

A Feather for Norma

Vickie Thompson

What is the odds so long as the fire of soul is kindled at the taper of conviviality, and the wing of friendship never moults a feather!
—Dickens, *The Olde Curiosity Shop*

IT GETS VERY HOT IN SAN ANTONIO AND I was impatiently waiting for the air conditioning to kick in as I pulled onto the main street in our sub-division. As I turned, I saw a sign for a garage sale. I had never been to a garage sale, had never even wanted to, but something made me turn around and head for it.

I parked and walked up the driveway, wondering why I was here to look at someone else's junk, when I noticed a car with Oklahoma plates. Having just moved to Texas from Oklahoma a few months earlier, I figured that even if I didn't find a bargain, I might find a kindred spirit. Little did I know then how prophetic that would be.

Norma was quite attractive in a flamboyant sort of way with platinum hair, two-inch finger-nails, and one-inch eyelashes, none of which she was born with. I guessed her to be around fifty. She was tall, slim, tan, and she waved her arms and hands about in that animated way that people do when they talk with their hands as much as their mouths.

We only talked a few minutes, but it was long enough to find out that we had lived about two miles from each other in Oklahoma City, were both natives of Missouri, and I was in serious need of baking dishes. I departed with an armload of baking dishes for fifty cents each. That evening after work, I walked back up the street. This time it was just to talk. That was ten years ago and we still haven't run out of things to talk about.

Norma became my best friend. Job transfers moved me to Atlanta, then to Connecticut. Norma moved to Las Vegas, then to Kansas City. We kept in touch by telephone and airplane. Last fall I made my first trip to Kansas City since Norma moved there. She had recently moved into a house, and I proposed we do a house "clearing."

House clearings are done to get rid of unwanted, stale, or negative energies and to help people make a special connection with their home. If occupants are tuned into the energy patterns, the home can develop a special feel, one that is noticeable to visitors. Many people have made comments to me like "I don't know what it is about your house. It just feels so peaceful."

At Norma's new home, we gathered all the materials we would need: candles, protection oils, smudge sticks made from sage and sweetgrass. We filled a jar with dried beans as a makeshift rattle. We started inside the house. Norma went into each room, using the rattle to break up stale energy around the walls and in the corners. I followed with a burning smudge stick to purify the rooms and drive out any unwanted energy.

For the second part of the ceremony, we moved outside. In my belief system, each direction is tied to an element: North is earth, East is air, South is fire, and West is water. First, we invoked the spirits of the North to come and provide protection. We did this in each direction, with Norma leaving a small gift of appreciation, something that represented the element symbolic of that direction. In the North, she left a favorite stone and in the East, an incense stick. A candle was given to the fiery South, and a seashell to the waters of the West.

Next, using essential oils, we drew protection symbols over each doorway and window, again asking for protection for the house and its inhabitants. Besides Norma, this was home to a sweet elderly dog named Tisha and two bashful Persian cats, Julio and Sinbad.

The next step was to surround the house with a circle of protection. I circled the house three times with a pot of burning sage to purify it. I continued around three more times, chanting and singing to invoke Goddess to come and create a protective circle of energy around the house. (Wisely, we chose to do this early on a Sunday morning before the neighbors started stirring!)

The protection part was important to me. Norma never realized how much I worried about her. She has extremely high blood pressure, and for years I carried around this fear that Norma would collapse in her kitchen, most likely from a stroke or heart attack. Irrationally, my fears never involved her having a problem in the bedroom, or living room, or bathroom. It was that darned kitchen that bothered me.

The final stage of a house blessing involves the owner connecting with the energy of the house itself. I asked Norma to go into each room, light a candle, and quietly "talk" to the room. She was to tell the room what she wanted from it. As an example, one might ask for peaceful sleep in a bedroom. People who have stressful jobs might go into their family room or den and ask the room to be a place where they can find tranquility and peace after a hectic day.

I don't know what Norma said in those rooms. I only know that as soon as she was out of sight, I grabbed a candle and headed for the kitchen. "Don't you dare let her die," I ordered.

The whole ceremony took about an hour and a half. Hot, sweaty, and drained of energy, we fixed big glasses of iced tea and retreated to the patio to recharge our batteries. Pretty soon we dragged ourselves out of the patio chairs and headed inside to clean up. After a long, relaxing shower, I wrapped my wet hair in a towel, put on a light robe, and walked across the hall to my bedroom.

As I walked toward the closet to get my clothes, something caught my eye. There, on the blue cushion of a small wicker chair sitting near the closet, was a small white feather. It was totally upright, the edge barely touching the cushion, as if it had floated down and was nearly weightless against the fabric.

My first thought was "Well, that's odd." Then it hit me. It was a message. The spirits I had called on to protect Norma were letting me know they had heard and things would be okay. I could stop worrying because she would be protected.

I went into Norma's bedroom and said, "Come here. I've got something to show you."

I guess I must have had a strange look on my face because she got very serious and followed me into the room. I pointed to the feather and she said, "Where did that come from?"

"I believe it came from the other side. I think it's a gift," I said.

She didn't say anything at first while she studied the feather. She assumed I had put it there and was waiting for me to explain what it meant.

"No, Norma. I didn't put it there," I said.

"Well, then, where did it come from?" she demanded again.

"I think it's a message," I said quietly. "I think it's their way of telling me that it worked. That they were listening."

She made a feeble attempt to rationalize it, but there was no way. Norma doesn't own a bird. There were no windows open anywhere, and I had been in and out of the room all morning and would have noticed it had it been there earlier.

I watched her face as she slowly realized what had happened. Her eyes got very big and her mouth fell open. I wish I could remember exactly what each of us said next, but all I really remember is feeling very exhilarated, very special. Norma built a small altar and placed the feather on it.

Four months later, Norma had a heart attack. I don't know if she was in the kitchen; I didn't ask. All I know is that the bargain was kept. She was protected and had a rapid recovery from heart surgery that corrected a serious blockage.

In a few weeks I'll be flying to Kansas City for another visit with Norma. We will talk and talk and go to some garage sales. We'll visit her kids and grandkids and then settle in and talk some more. We'll drink coffee and read the newspaper on the patio in the early morning hours. We'll do all the normal things that lifetime friends do.

And in that peaceful time just before dawn,
I will go outside and connect with She
    who is watching.
I will honor the spirits of the elements.
I will offer my deepest thanks for keeping
    watch.
And I will wear feathers in my hair. 🪶

Ritual

A HOUSE BLESSING WITH FEATHERS

A house blessing can be done when you move into a home, or whenever you feel the need to cleanse and purify it. In my household, we perform a house blessing once a year, usually around the fall equinox.

* For your house blessing, you may want to invite friends to bring their own feathers. They may accompany you as you walk through the rooms and around the perimeter of the house, strengthening and enforcing your own motions. Or you can ask each of them to take a room and lead the blessing in that room.

* If you have a special prayer feather or feather bundle, use it in the blessing. If not, choose your most powerful feather and spend some time in meditation with it, claiming the intention that it assist in sweeping away negative or stale energies and bringing in new and protective energies.

* Taking your feather, walk around the perimeter of each room, sweeping with the feather. Pay special attention to the corners, where stale energy can collect.

* Pause at each door and window opening, making your own prayers of protection and blessing, asking that each entryway be reinforced with the energies of the Spirit.

* End your ceremony by traveling the perimeter of the house, pausing at each of the four directions to honor the natural environment surrounding and supporting your home.

You may want to leave small feathers in each room, as a convenient way to cleanse and renew the energy whenever you wish.

Joined Energies

Toby Evans

THE GREAT HORNED OWL CAME TO ME AS MY primary totem in my first shamanic journey to the lower world. I was fascinated by the owl's medicine described by the Chumash Indian woman, Choqosh Auh-ho-oh, as "the transformer, the one that sees the light in the darkness." The owl, she said, represents death of the ego and death of confusion of all that is out of balance. This powerful energy is not always easy to be around.

At that point in my life, I was co-directing a church youth education program with a woman named Debbie. We were involved in a drumming group and our spiritual goals led us to integrate Medicine Wheel teachings into our Oneness with All Life youth curriculum. Eventually, we developed a workshop for adults and were invited to travel back to my hometown to present it.

Only an hour into the drive, we saw a dead bird in the road, its wing lifting to catch our attention. Stopping, we found ourselves staring into the large golden eyes of a great horned owl. The body was in perfect shape, and we knew this was a gift we were honored to accept.

When we arrived, we asked and received Owl's permission to remove the wings. We decided that each of us would take one. I agreed to dry and prepare them when we got home. During the curing process, I heard an inner message: "The wings are a symbol of your partnership together and the work you are to do. When that work is over, you will need to return the wings to the earth."

I didn't like this message. I was already attached to my wing and more attached to my relationship with Debbie. We were just at a beginning point and the idea of an ending didn't appeal to me. I filed the words away in a back mind-closet, content to forget that I ever heard them.

Over the next four years, Debbie and I continued to join our energies in weekly planning sessions for our church school program. Our partnership expanded into sharing our Medicine workshops with teachers and students in public schools. Owl seemed to be with us, gliding on the air currents, taking us into deeper areas of inner and outer work. We used the wings in our own ways, including healing sessions and personal rituals, but eventually our lives began to take separate directions.

I was restless, feeling pulled back to my land and to my art. It seemed that my karmic contract with the church had been fulfilled and I was ready to leave. At the same time, Debbie's mom, Della, had been diagnosed with cancer and Debbie spent much of the end time at her side. I agreed to remain with the program until she could return. We didn't know that Della's death would also signify our completion.

After Della died, we both resigned and

Debbie's life was transformed into taking on the duties of her mother. She brought her father into her home and became his constant caretaker. I had less and less contact with her, although we continued to meet in the drumming group. We didn't talk about the dissolution of our partnership, although it was apparent that we were moving in different directions.

When the owl would come to me in shamanic journeys, I would begin by riding on its back. But sometimes I would find myself sitting in the windowsill of a huge round opening, watching the night stars glide by, and I would realize that I was riding in the eye of the owl. Often, when the journey was over, I would return to normal size and look back to see my companion rotate his head, staring deeply into my soul. The golden pools of light in his eyes changed to sapphire-blue and the feathers turned stark white.

The likeness was similar to my large white Himalayan cat that came to me from a family member with the name, Rainbow. I would wake up in the middle of the night and see him perched on our headboard. His white fur glowed silver, illuminated by the moonlight as he looked longingly outside. In those moments, he was always an owl to me.

Late in the fall, Rainbow went for his usual romp in the yard. It was after dark when I realized that he hadn't come back. Calling for him, I received the answering hoot of an owl. An uneasy feeling moved within me.

The next morning I discovered what the owl had already reported. Rainbow was found dead in the road, killed by a car. I placed him within the Medicine Wheel area on our property. When I went in to tell Adam, my eleven-year-old son, he was very upset and asked to stay home from school. I assured him we would do a ceremony together for Rainbow before burying him at the base of a large cedar tree.

Adam sat on the ground crying, clutching Rainbow's limp body in his arms while I went to get my sage, tobacco, and owl wing. When we finished our ritual, I placed his body into the hole we had dug and then heard clear instructions in my mind: "And now it is time to also bury your wing. Place it over Rainbow's body. The partnership between you and Debbie is over and it's time to release this."

I viewed this as the announcement of another death and everything in me resisted while knowing I had to comply. It was difficult to tell Debbie that my half of the wings was buried. It wasn't up to me to insist that she bury hers. She knew my initial instructions and she wasn't ready.

Several years went by and Debbie's life was consumed with family demands. The owl wing was tucked into a closet and never used. Finally, she decided to sell her house and move to another state, but it was not an easy process. Things kept getting derailed. The momentum would build and then come to a screeching halt.

Just before Mother's Day, I phoned Debbie on impulse to find out how she was doing. Her father had recently moved into a care facility. She asked me if I thought it was possible to take on another's karma because she suspected that Della had been with her all this time!

After hanging up the phone, I felt Della by my side. She told me that she had joined her energy with Debbie since dying because of her need to work out unfinished issues with her husband, but she assured me that it was with Debbie's consent.

I recalled that shortly after Della's death, Debbie shared a dream with me in which Della came to her and asked if she could be her. Debbie didn't know what she meant. Della explained it would be like wearing her clothes for a while. Not knowing what she was agreeing to, Debbie told her mother she would help. Shortly afterward, I watched Debbie gain weight and take on new aches and pains that she didn't have before. Physically, she resembled Della more and more.

Della was now indicating that the work was complete and she was ready to move on, ready to let Debbie pursue her own life. She wasn't exactly trapped between the two worlds, but she had grown attached to Debbie's body and knew that in order to release it, she was going to need some assistance. I relayed this to Debbie, and we agreed to create a ceremony to help her. The logical part of me didn't have a clue how to proceed, but I trusted that the directions would come and all we would have to do was follow them.

The instructions I received were to use something that had belonged to Della and to have Debbie bring a cassette tape of "The Fairy Ring" and her owl wing. I had a woven cloth from Della that I kept in my art studio along with many skeins of colored ribbon that she had once used for decorating and sewing.

On Mother's Day, Debbie lay down in the middle of my studio floor with a tall wooden stepladder set up over her body. She looked as if she were lying beneath a giant compass or a teepee. On the top rung of the ladder, I placed a white candle; below it was a bowl of dried flowers. I placed a purple candle at Debbie's head holding the alignment to Spirit, and a green candle at her feet to represent her connection to Earth. At the very top of the ladder, I laid out the woven cloth and positioned the owl wing on top of it.

Taking the ribbon, I was shown the areas on Debbie's physical body where Della's energy-spirit held on. I ceremoniously tied one color at a time around each spot—around her wrists, ankles, waist, chest, throat, and forehead. From each point, I pulled the ribbon skyward by climbing to the top of the ladder. Up and down I went until all of the spots were attached to the owl wing resting on the top rung. It created a maypole effect.

With everything in place I turned on the "Fairy Ring" music and began working with Della, coaxing her out of Debbie's body. At first nothing seemed to be happening. I circled Debbie, calling in guides and angels and asking for Owl's assistance. He was to be Della's chariot, flying between the middle and the upper world, taking her home.

Within a few moments, Della's spirit sat straight up out of Debbie's waist, calling, "Ruth, you have to help me!" Ruth was her deceased sister. At once Ruth was there, along with other helpers. I watched them support Della on all sides. In unison, we reassured Della that it was time to leave. Slowly, she began to lift out of Debbie's solar plexus. Her spirit was following the ribbons as circuits of her own life energy. Della was being pulled up the ladder, rung by rung. The aroma of the flowers greeted her and she paused, telling me that I needed to place the flowers at Debbie's head and feet. She waited for me to sprinkle some in both areas before she spoke again.

"Just give me a moment to settle into the owl wing." When she was ready she continued, "Now cut the ribbons. This is harder for me to let go than it was when I died."

I moved to Debbie with a pair of scissors, deliberately snipping each ribbon, sensing that I was severing the energetic passageway back into her body. Every fragment of the sliced ribbon-cords had to be removed and the openings into those areas sealed off on the etheric level. The long dangling pieces that remained hanging down from the owl wing were pulled up and tucked underneath it. Symbolically, all of Della's circuits were returned to her before I was told to tend to Debbie.

Debbie's motionless body was carefully wrapped in a sheet with a baby blanket tucked around her. Another set of helpers had arrived with her restoration in mind. There was a mummy-wrapping action of pure energy spinning from her feet up to her head. The purpose was to squeeze any residue of Della out of Debbie's solar plexus area. When this process was complete, Debbie and I wrapped the wing and all the gathered ribbon tightly into the underlying cloth and took it to the East pole of the Four Directional Gates positioned outside my Medicine Wheel.

I placed the owl wing into the prepared hole, and we bid Della good-bye, freeing the true essence of her spirit.

The long passage with Owl taught Debbie and me about death on many levels, guiding us through the darkness we found within ourselves and others by finding the beacon of our own inner light. We will be forever grateful to Owl who divided himself to join our energies. In the process of bringing his wings back together, we were freed to go our separate ways, bonded in the truth of our wholeness. ✑

Spirit Messenger

Will Davis

A FEW YEARS AGO I WAS GOING THROUGH A rough time in my life. I had ended an important relationship, one that I thought would lead to marriage. I had been praying for guidance ever since, but it seemed as though no one was listening.

One day as I was leaving work I stood outside my car, waiting in the large parking lot for my friend, Sonny, who rides with me every day. I saw him come out of the back entrance, so I turned to get into the car.

Suddenly I saw a large hawk flying in my direction. I didn't pay a lot of attention at first, until the hawk for some reason swooped down directly toward me. Just before it reached where I was standing—about ten feet away—it banked sharply upward again. As it did, a feather from its wing fell right between my feet.

I stared at the feather with a feeling of wonder. The feather was in perfect condition and beautifully shaped. Sonny came running up. He couldn't contain his excitement.

"Did you see that? Did you see that?" he kept saying.

Still looking at the feather, I replied, "That was amazing. He just swooped down on me. I don't know if it was me or if it saw something . . .

but look at this feather it dropped, it's beautiful!"

I picked up the feather, took it home, and laid it on a table. Later that evening I picked it up and held it in my hands, seeing again in my mind how miraculously this feather had come to me. "Maybe it's a sign," I thought. "I'll pray with this feather."

After I prayed, I made a small shield with a piece of elk hide and attached the feather to the center of it.

The next day, I started feeling better. Within the next couple of weeks, I felt healed and ready to move on. Eventually I found someone even better suited to share my life with me, someone who is interested in walking the same spiritual path.

I still have that small shield with the feather in the center. In some Native American beliefs, the hawk is known as the messenger, and I believe that the Creator sent me a message that day, that everything would be all right, that no matter what you're handed that seems bad or negative, you're also given much that is good.

Whenever I'm not in a good place with myself or with my world, no matter where I am, I can picture that hawk swooping down and leaving a feather for me, and I hear its message again. ❧

Owning My Power

Carol Rydell

WHEN I WAS FOUR YEARS OLD, I WASN'T HAPPY being here in the physical world. In my confusion, I tried numerous times to escape the heaviness of my body and the family that I had chosen to be with.

In trying to escape the bewilderment and density, I experienced three major accidents in the same year. The third was life threatening. I was chasing my younger sister, as siblings do. She locked me out of the house. I began knocking on the French door leading from our living room to the screened-in porch, crying for her to let me in. I knocked and knocked to no avail, until suddenly my arm crashed through the glass pane.

It was a severe injury. After more than 250 stitches in my upper arm and eight blood transfusions, I lay resting in my hospital bed in the children's ward. Lying directly to the right of my bed was a girl just two years older. People constantly hovered around her. A rattlesnake had bitten her and she was very ill.

I remember not being afraid of my own injury, but afraid, instead, of the trauma that my wardmate was going through. The fear and concern of her family, doctors, and nurses frightened me. This snake frightened me. It must have been a horrid creature to do this to her.

Forty years after my arm injury, I still thought of that horrible snake. I felt deep within myself that it was time to come to terms with my fear. Logically, it was not justified.

After many years of cross-cultural spiritual studies, I came to perceive the snake as a symbol of transmutation, the process of death and rebirth. A snake sheds its skin moving from life to death back to new life, just as we shed the old parts of ourselves to be born again, beginning a new cycle of our own life.

Reflecting on my fear of the snake, I realized that I was afraid of shedding those parts of myself that no longer served me in the way they had done so lovingly for many years. It was time to shed my old skin. Not long after my reflections, the universe graciously presented me with an opportunity.

I was on my way to a doctor's appointment. It was a lovely spring day. I loved to drive through the park to watch the geese on the ponds and the wildlife that might also appear. As I rounded a curve, there lying on the side of the road was a snake. It appeared to be dead. As soon as I saw it, I knew that it was there for me. Feeling anxious, I stopped to look at it, knowing that it was dead but feeling nonetheless frightened.

"Take the snake home with you," I heard an inner voice say. I couldn't believe what I was hearing, but I knew that it was true.

"That's crazy," my pragmatic self replied, "just because there's a dead snake on the road doesn't mean you have to pick it up."

I decided to go on to the doctor's office so that I wouldn't be late for my appointment. If that snake were really mine to do something with, it would be waiting for me when I returned.

As the doctor left the examining room, I heard myself ask his assistant if I could have a pair of the rubber surgical gloves that were in a box hanging on the wall.

"Sure, what do you need them for?" she asked.

"I'm working on a project that is messy," I said. "I just need one pair."

She told me to go ahead and take them. I thanked her and was on my way. I felt ridiculous.

As I drove through the park once again, I knew the snake would still be waiting for me. I never thought of taking another route home so that I didn't have to encounter the dilemma. As I approached the same curve in the road, there it was. It hadn't moved an inch.

It was in beautiful condition. I'm not even sure how it died because it didn't appear to have any injuries. It felt like further confirmation that I was to take the snake home with me.

I slowly got out of my car, still afraid that the snake would somehow come to life and injure me. Cars cautiously passed me, trying to determine what was going on. When I stood next to the snake, it appeared larger than I realized. It was between three and four feet long and it was solid black. How would I get it home with me? I opened the trunk of my car, found a plastic bag from the grocery store, and put on the surgical gloves.

I couldn't do it. My heart was pounding, my knees shaking and my breath rapid. I told myself that I must do this. It was time for me to come to terms with my fear once and for all. Again I looked in my car for something that could help me. A golf club—this was the snake-handling tool I needed.

"Now you look really ridiculous," my critical-parent voice chimed in. "The trunk of your car is open. You have surgical gloves on and a golf club and plastic bag in your hands. What will people driving by think?"

I didn't care. Slowly I picked up the snake with my "special tool" and lowered it into the plastic bag I was holding. I dumped it into my trunk. I could hardly catch my breath.

Driving home, I began to shake. I've never felt so foolish. When I arrived, I used my trusty tool to take the plastic bag out of my trunk and carry it to the backyard. I emptied the bag into my flower garden where I stretched out the snake next to the glistening quartz crystals lining the garden borders. As I stood admiring my gift from the universe, I still felt fear, but I also felt admiration, pride, and accomplishment.

Hurriedly I went through the sliding door into the kitchen to call a friend and share this experience. After ten minutes on the phone, I went outside and almost fell over in disbelief. Lying directly at the head of my snake was a beautiful dead blue jay with both wings completely spread open.

Blue jays have always entered my life when I need to recognize or give honor to my own power or to properly use my power. I took this as a sign from the universe that I had just gone through a powerful symbolic experience, facing my fear head-on.

Normally, I would have taken both creatures and buried them immediately, but I found myself wanting to admire them lying together. The day grew into night, and still I had not put them to rest by performing a burial ceremony.

The next morning, the bright sun warmed me as I walked outside onto the deck. I had prepared myself emotionally and spiritually to do the ceremony that I had not done the day before. I stood on my deck and glanced into the garden. Both the snake and the blue jay were gone.

I panicked. My first feelings were of guilt. I didn't perform ceremony as I should have and therefore they had been taken from me. I searched everywhere I could think of: under the deck, around the house, in the entire yard. Maybe my cat or an opossum or raccoon took them down to the creek next to my land. After searching the creek beds, the snake and blue jay were still nowhere to be found.

I decided to do a burial ceremony for them, even though they were no longer with me physically. I said prayers of thanks for the gifts and teachings that they shared. I offered water, tobacco, and corn-meal to Mother Earth.

Early the following morning I had a dream. I was shown that the snake was under the deck and ready to come back now. Although I had looked under there thoroughly the day before, I leaped out of bed, threw on some clothes, went to the garage, and got the long piece of wood with nails protruding from it that I'd used the day before to reach under the deck.

I knelt by the stairs of the deck and began to poke and prod. Suddenly I felt something heavy. I pulled and there was the snake, on the end of the piece of wood. My snake was back. I reflected on just how magical life is.

I didn't waste any time performing a burial ceremony. My guidance instructed me to stretch the snake out perfectly straight in a channel dug in the earth and put rocks over it. The Earth Mother and her creatures would do what they do and, after two or three months, I was to remove the vertebrae of the snake to be used in the jewelry and art that I create. Once again I said prayers and offered tobacco, water, and cornmeal.

It was a glorious morning, and I went for my daily walk. I felt so full of gratitude for what had already occurred that morning. After walking for about twenty minutes, I turned a corner and there in front of me lying next to the road was a blue jay feather. I bent over and picked it up.

It was magnificently colored, blue and black

with white accents on the tip. Immediately I heard that it came to me as a gift of *honor and reciprocity*. Since I had honored the blue jay without its physical form, it was honoring me with its presence. I was thankful for this gift and said a prayer of gratitude as I again started walking, holding the feather in my hand.

In the grass to my left, I saw another blue jay feather. I leaned over and picked it up. It was as beautiful as the first. It said that it came to me as the gift of *death and rebirth*, a continuous cycle. Symbolically I had experienced this cycle when I chose to embrace my fear of the snake.

I continued my walk and there was yet another feather for me. As I held this one, I heard that it carried the gift of *faith*, letting me know that I am not alone in this process.

Another feather appeared; this one brought the gift of understanding that *the nonphysical world is as powerful as the physical*. I had performed a ceremony even when I thought I no longer had the snake or the bird to bury. They knew of the honoring.

Every fifteen to twenty feet, another feather gifted itself to me, each bringing its unique message. The final feather said that it came as a gift of *owning my own power*. I no longer chose to give an old fear any power over me. I was told that the single, most important thing we can do in the world is to become the most of who we are and are meant to be.

By the time I returned, I had gathered twenty-two feathers in all. My sacred bird had been returned to me, but in a different form. I took the feathers to the snake's burial spot and laid all but one feather atop the freshly turned earth.

The single blue jay feather that I kept resides respectfully on my desk at home. Every time I look at it, I reflect on the precious gifts feathers can offer. As I continue to grow spiritually and emotionally, becoming more fully who I am, I have a deeper understanding of their messages. ✑

A Little White Feather

Cate M. Cummings

IT IS OCTOBER. I STARE DOWN AT MY FATHER'S driver's license. I hold it and try to visualize, on this small, precise government-issue card, the dimension of a man's life. I am trying to keep in mind, as I sit in the hospital waiting room with my husband consoling me, that the man who is my father, lying in an ICU unit close by with five bodily systems shut down, deserves more consideration and deliberation than the doctors are giving him. Apparently it is my burden because I will not pronounce my father done.

How in the world, though, do I make these decisions? The doctors want permission to remove the breathing tube from the tracheotomy, the feeding tube from his stomach, the dialysis equipment persuading his kidneys to continue functioning . . . and on . . . and on. The hospital staff, having given up on my father and pronounced him "ready to pass on," is goading me to free up space for someone who has a chance, a *real* chance of being "fixed."

It is November. Sometimes, when I walk the halls of the hospital building, I feel as if I am in a surreal moment—dreamlike if you will, nightmarish if you'd rather. All the floors of the building are exactly alike—distinguished only by the elevator buttons I push in a daze of despair. This morning, once again, my husband and I walk along the never-ending corridor in shadowed light toward the ICU double doors that do not welcome us but serve as barriers. As we reach the doors, I become aware of something on the floor in front of us.

There we are—in the hospital corridor in front of the double doors, both bending to pick up the little white feather we see lying on the floor. A little white feather! A feather in a sterile hospital environment!?

"I think it's for you," my husband says impulsively.

Puzzled, holding the feather in my hand, I begin to move through the doors. As I look up again, I am astonished to realize we are not on the fourth floor ICU unit but on the second floor. Together, we hold the little white feather as we read in huge letters on the glass door in front of us—DELIVERY. It is the place where babies are born, where hope is born, where new life—new life!—becomes a reality.

In the midst of chiding relatives urging me to give up on my father, my father's own living trust stating "do not use extraordinary measures to keep me alive in the event of a medical catastrophe," the medical staff's inexplicable lack of faith in any type of recovery at all, I was immutable. I insisted on not deciding to take a life. I decided to persist, to endure, to persevere, to choose life. Not the cliché "life," but life as a never-to-be-seen-again version of, an extraordinary expression of, that benefactor we cannot really name.

The gift of mind is an immense blessing bestowed upon us; and, sometimes with a hint to create a stir in our mind's moment, we wake up and come to understand that we are being soothed in the warmed gloved hand of God as we might protect a small fragile bird or its feather in our own hands.

It is December. In a few more days, it will be Christmas. My father is here in my home visiting with me. "DELIVERY!"

Meditation

FEATHER COLORS AND WHAT THEY MEAN

Throughout history, feathers have symbolized different things in different cultures. Nevertheless, many feather colors have been seen to have near-universal meanings.

When a feather comes to you, take note of its color, its shape, size, type, and origin. Open yourself to any messages that may come to you.

- **Blue feathers** bring peace, protection, a sense of well-being. Blue jay feathers can also bring warnings of trouble ahead.
- **Black feathers** are a symbol of mystical wisdom from spiritual initiation. They can also be a warning sign of ill health, death, or transition immediately ahead.
- **Brown feathers** bring stability, dignity, and respect.
- **Brown feathers with black stripes or bars** symbolize balance between the physical and spiritual.
- **Green feathers** are a symbol of renewal, new directions, and new growth.
- **Iridescent feathers (flashes of shiny colors)** are a symbol of mystical insight, wholeness, spiritual transcendence. Peacock feathers can also be a warning against false pride.
- **Red feathers** bring vitality and health. Polynesian and South American tribes saw red feathers as symbols for the earth, blood, and femaleness. Royalty wore red feather headdresses and capes; coils of red feathers known as "red feather money," were traded for various needs. The great Mayan "feathered serpent" god, Quetzalcoatl, had the red beak of a bird as a mouth.
- **White feathers** are a symbol of purification, love, innocence, and new life.
- **Yellow feathers** symbolize cheerfulness, mental alertness, and prosperity, the sun, and maleness.

Spirit of Owl

Raven Lamoreux-Dodd

THE KNEES OF THE CYPRESS TREES ROSE OUT of the brackish water like sentinels, surveying the misty greens and grays of the Everglades. A dusky blue heron stepped gingerly on the wild lettuce, not wanting to disturb the alligator beneath. His long beak tested the swamp for food. I stood on the boardwalk listening, waiting, and watching. A woodpecker startled me. The heron lifted majestically into the mists as the lettuce moved mysteriously; then we all settled down again.

The sunset cast an eerie glow through the tendrils of Spanish moss hanging from gnarled branches. I sensed a new presence and turned in time to see a barred owl swooping down the boardwalk toward me. Its wingspan seemed enormous, and I wondered how the owl could navigate in the thick tropical forest. As I was about to duck, she rose to a branch just above me and contemplated me. I gazed into pools of dark chocolate filled with compassion, and the ecstasy in my heart and throat was almost unbearable. The love in her eyes contained the whole universe. I wanted to acknowledge her and communicate my love for her as well.

I felt honored and deeply grateful for her visit. Leaning toward me, she began to make noises and motion with her beak. I breathed deeply to calm myself so that I could hear. The message was one of support and kinship. Then, as sounds of other humans drifted through the leaves, she glanced in their direction, back at me, and lifted into the dark canopy without a sound.

Since that time, owls have been a constant spirit presence in my life. Owl is always there when I am about to work or when I need help or inspiration. Whatever country I live in or visit, the owls fly with me and appear to me. At our home in England, owls call to us at night and in the morning.

Perhaps the most consistent message from Owl to me has been, "Trust your inner knowing." That message was present the night I received an extraordinary gift from a dying owl.

As I left the Micossukee Indian reservation to return home one night, the new moon cast only a glimmer of encouragement. The two-lane highway seemed unusually narrow in the darkness, its white lines flashing by at seventy miles an hour. My thoughts were filled with the day's experiences, and I concentrated on the truck in front of me to help me drive. Suddenly, I glimpsed a movement to the left of the truck, barely perceptible in the vehicle's lights. It was an owl, and it was flying too low. I stared in horror as it collided with the truck and crashed onto the right shoulder. I slowed the car and pulled over. Still shaken, I waited for a group of cars to pass before trying to open the door. "Great Spirit," I called, "please help me." A check of the trunk revealed no flashlight, but I did find my Aztec blanket.

Aided by the lights of a few more passing cars, I walked the long distance back to the owl. The traffic disappeared. I could barely see the steel rails between the fence posts, and the mists were rising. I continued praying for help and tried to "see" through my feet. I must have gone a couple of hundred yards when I heard an owl hoot. I stopped and listened. It was a barred owl; its mournful throaty call sent shivers down my spine.

As another car passed, I looked down at my feet and saw the owl lying on the ground before me. I asked for permission to touch the bird and carefully moved it to see if it was alive. Its neck had been broken. I lifted it onto the blanket, talking to its spirit and asking Great Spirit to care for it. The owl that had been hooting called once more. What was I to do?

I felt strongly that I should take the owl home. I sensed that I would receive further guidance on the way. I left an offering of tobacco and walked back to the car. I felt strangely elated, afraid, and confident all at once.

In the car, I talked to the owl and stroked its head as I drove. Once home, I wondered what I was doing with this owl and what right I had to take it from the swamp. From deep within a voice said, "You may keep the wings and claws and take some of the feathers from the heart area. Bury the rest of the owl in the proper way near where you do ceremony. Once you have completed these things, you will know what to do with them."

I was deeply grateful for this opportunity although not sure how to proceed. I made a cup of coffee, turned off the lights, and sat with the owl. Gazing into the night sky, I began to prepare myself to care for its beautiful body.

The balmy Gulf breeze drifted in through the window, stirring me into action. I knew that I didn't have much time if I was going to preserve the wings in their open, flying position. I had some experience with cleaning partridges from living in the Quebec countryside. Although I had always cleaned and eaten partridges with respect and had used their feathers in an honorable way, this was quite different. At 1:00 A.M. I was hesitant to call anyone for advice, so for now I had to rely on messages from Spirit and myself.

I took a shower and cleansed the owl, the room, and myself with burning sage. As I removed the wings, I asked the owl for forgiveness if I did anything to dishonor it. I removed the flesh from the wing bones with a scalpel. When I had cleaned them as well as I could, I opened the wings to full span, attached them to oven racks with wooden clothespins, and placed them in the warm oven. I turned the oven off and left the door open. While the wings were drying, I collected the claws and the chest feathers and wrapped them in a red cotton cloth to protect them.

I glanced at the clock, astonished that it was

now 6:00 A.M. I decided to call a Native American friend to ask his advice about how to get the last bits of flesh off the wings. I knew that Owl is a powerful medicine to have and therefore felt a great responsibility to do honor to its carcass.

He advised me to call upon the ants for help. If I placed the wings somewhere that the ants could get at them without foxes, skunks, or other creatures interfering, they would solve my problem. Of course I would have to keep watch and stop the ants at the right time.

Imagining the reactions of the neighbors if I hung the wings from my window, I said it was impossible! Finally, I put the wings on the screened porch, since the ants were small enough to get in through the screen.

A couple of days later, my friend joined me. We dusted and cleaned the wings and then asked the ants to go home. I was pleased to see that they had no wish to stay. I buried the owl in a sacred spot with offerings of tobacco and cornmeal, and prayers, asking for the blessings of Great Spirit and of the owl. I was told to use the wings to dance. "Dance to heal yourself and to help others. Dance to journey with Owl and see through the darkness. Owl will always be with you."

I am deeply grateful for Owl's gifts of Spirit. Each time I dance with the beautiful owl feathers, I remember the message to "trust your inner knowing" as I continue my healing journey. ✑

Feathers and Dolls

Vicki Wagoner

IN A CHILDHOOD OFTEN PLAGUED WITH abuse, I had two dolls that were constant companions. I clung to them in an effort to pretend that my childhood was "normal." One of the dolls was a flexible cloth doll with a brightly painted face. The other was a hard plastic bridal doll, with a solemn look about her eyes and a pouty mouth. I thought they were the most beautiful dolls ever made.

One day, years later, as I was cleaning my closet, I found them. I decided that it was time for them to go, but I didn't want to throw them in the trash. They had been part of me, part of my childhood, as awful and sad as it was at times.

I realized I had to bury them, but where, I didn't know. I carried them in my car, along with a small shovel, knowing that one day I would be guided.

Several weeks went by. One weekend afternoon, I drove to a beachside park. I had not been there for years, never had a strong desire to go there, yet I knew that this was the place and now was the time to complete my mission.

I gathered the dolls, wrapped them in a beach towel, took my shovel, and headed to the beach. I didn't know where I was going to bury them, but I knew I would be guided. I walked for a short while, then stopped, sat on the sand, and began to dig. I put the tip of the shovel into the sand and there, right at the tip of the shovel, was a small white feather—confirmation for me that this was the place. I pocketed the gift, smiled, silently said a prayer of thanks, and kept digging.

I dug a small hole, just large enough for the dolls. I put a shell in their hands. I forgave my past, said good-bye, and thanked God and the angels for helping me have the strength to do this. Filling the hole with sand, I said a silent prayer of farewell.

I decided to go into the Gulf to cleanse myself with the saltwater. As I walked toward the water I looked down; at my feet was a large beige feather. I picked it up, said another prayer of thanks, put it with the white one, and walked back to the water. I submerged my whole self in the water, releasing old hurts, asking to be cleansed and filled with light.

Suddenly, there were birds swooping and landing in the water all around me. I felt protected and loved. It seemed that the angels were coming to me in the form of birds!

I emerged from the water, dried off, and started to leave the beach when once again at my feet was a large chocolate brown feather. This time I started laughing, and finally, the tears came, too, tears of relief and satisfaction that another part of my past had been healed.

Dancing Feathers

Stumbling Deer

FOR YEARS, I HAD DREAMS WITH FEATHERS. These feathers came into my dreams as a tool of spiritual guidance. Barred feathers appeared first. In another dream, I saw twin kachinas with blossoms of blue jay feathers on each side of their heads walking east across my lawn after a spring rain.

One dream kept repeating. In this dream, I was a pilot going through a gate at the airport. I saw lots of black feathers, which I picked up and put into a briefcase. I said, "This one is broken — too bad — but maybe it's still usable." I gathered all the feathers I saw, broken and unbroken, and put them into the briefcase.

It was time to find out the meaning of the dream. I visited Bear Butte, South Dakota, with two friends. We met in a sacred area known and respected by all tribes and began a vision quest. We each took a different path up the butte to let the Great Spirit speak to us. I found a place partway up the side of the butte, hidden among the evergreens.

I had carried a horsehide with me because I expected some cold weather. But I didn't expect the extremes of weather we had. During the quest, I experienced every kind of weather but snow. Rain pelted down, then turned into freezing sleet and hail. I hunkered over on my knees to stay warm, but eventually I went unconscious from the cold. Then I saw an old Native American man, one who had appeared to me before in dreams and visions.

"Wake up or you'll die," he said.

I immediately opened my eyes, but I couldn't stop shivering. I thought I would freeze to death, literally. Then a woman's voice gently commanded me to sing. "You've got to be kidding," I protested. But she insisted, so I started chanting. Instantly, I warmed up, and I knew I would make it through without freezing.

Seven days later, I had another dream. I was in a high stone tower with a friend, looking out of the west window. The tower was standing over all of the world, and I was looking down at everything that was going on. It was a beautiful spring day, and I could see all the plowed earth. I wore only a knee-length buckskin cloth wrapped around my waist.

I turned to my dream friend and said, "It's time to go down." I put a large black feather head-dress on. The feathers, I realized, were those I had collected in my previous dreams, and they were attached to a red headband. I put the headdress on and went out to dance.

Then, in the dream, my grandfather (who is part Cherokee) came to me and showed me a stone arch and a stone medicine wheel. In the center was a large water fountain. He told me I was to re-create this vision and create a ritual that would be similar to the Sun Dance, but without the ritual chest piercings. It would be called the Stone Dance.

I understood, finally, the dream of black feathers. For me, black is the color of the North direction, the direction of winter. All of my spiritual connections begin in the North. My birth date is in December; my spiritual birth took place in the North, in the Saskatchewan territory. The North is the place of wisdom, of inner seeing and knowing. It is the place of nonjudgment, the place where you forgive yourself and others, and dwell only in the present. It is also a symbol for the feminine, the darkness, going back into the womb.

The dream offered me the time to be consciously born into my full medicine powers, anointing me with both the red energy (South, masculine) and the black energy (North, feminine).

Last year I led the ninth Stone Dance in a sacred wooded area dedicated for that purpose each spring. Each year I teach those who want to dance how to receive the sacred energy from the Creator that will empower them to make the next step in their journey.

The dream vision of dancing black feathers has been fulfilled. ✺

The Earth Is a Perfect Mother

Rod Skenandore, Ph.D., "Elk Chief"

*When all the trees have burned and died and only
stumps remain,
We'll come out from our hideaway and we'll start to
pray for rain.
The rain will fill the riverbeds and make the saplings
grow
And we'll plant seeds the eagle brings and we'll pray
back the snow.
And we'll pray back the robin, the elk, the snake, the
dove,
And we'll pray back the meadowlark, the one who
carries love.*
—excerpts from *The Earth Is a Perfect Mother*,
by Rod Skenandore, Ph.D., "Elk Chief"

AS A MEMBER OF THE BLACKFEET/ONEIDA tribe and a lifelong spiritual leader and healer, I know that feathers are sacred tools. They express our intention. They are one of the ways Spirit speaks directly to those who listen. As the ancient prophecies have set forth, it is time to open the doors between peoples, between worlds, and let the earth be healed.

When I ask for a connection with Spirit, an eagle comes. Eagle feathers have dropped down from the air to me. When my wife was pregnant with our daughter, we headed west into the mountains of Wyoming and came across a group of pinto burros. We stopped to admire them, and I took my eagle fan out of the car and began fanning them, blessing them for their labors. Suddenly, an eagle appeared directly above us. We watched as it circled and dropped a feather. I caught it in midair. It was a small feather, representing the child we would soon have, and it was Spirit's message that all would go well with the birth.

I took my feathers with me into federal court, to help defend the right of Native Americans to perform the Sun Dance as a religious ceremony. All charges were dismissed against us. We then filed suit against the federal government for religious persecution. This landmark case eventually led to the Native American Freedom of Religion Act.

I wore my eagle feather into the Omaha, Nebraska courtroom where two of my companions, members of the American Indian Movement we had founded to reclaim political and civil rights for Native Americans, were on trial for murdering FBI agents at the Pine Ridge Reservation. I watched in silence as the head of the CIA admitted, on cross-examination, that he had lied about the evidence. When I came out of the courtroom, reporters asked me how I felt the trial was going.

"It will be over in two days," I replied. Since the trial had been expected to go on for weeks, this was a rather amazing prediction. But the signs from Spirit were clear.

I drove to the outskirts of town and headed

my car out into the countryside. When I reached the right spot, I got out, carrying my tobacco and my eagle feather with me. I prayed and performed a ceremony for my captive brothers. In this altered state, I had a vision of a large bundle of eagle feathers piled on top of the scales of justice carved into the stone entrance of the Omaha courthouse. The scales were equally balanced. Mentally, I reached out and placed my eagle feather on one side, the side I knew as "truth." The scale tipped down, outweighing the other side. Two days later, as I had predicted, my companions were acquitted.

The most dire circumstances can be healed with the feather's sacred healing power. With prayer and ceremony, with the feather to express the shaman's intention, anything desired can happen. One example is the Uwipi ceremony, a sacred healing ceremony in the Lakota Sioux tradition.

An altar is created with symbols of the four directions and a person is tied, hands behind his back, ropes binding his limbs. A blanket completely covers the shaman's bound body. The space is darkened and the ceremony begins. Only Spirit can untie the blanketed man. Only Spirit has the power to loosen the knots and release us from problems we have created for ourselves.

In one Uwipi ceremony, we gathered in a large room. We placed blankets over all the windows to darken the room even more. Those gathered sat in a large circle around the room. They chanted and drummed, waiting for spirit energies to gather. I waited under the blanket, my bonds wrapped tight against my arms, legs, and chest. The darkness was stifling.

Suddenly, I heard ancient healing songs coming out of the dark and my bonds loosened until I could easily slip out of them. In front of me appeared the souls of seven elders, seated in a semicircle around me. I sat there with them, absorbing their power and energy.

They glowed with light. On the altar behind them was a large eagle feather on a wheel with streamers, which had been worn by Crow Dog. I watched the feather as it rose up by itself, surrounded by light, and traveled across the room toward me with its own shimmering energy.

Tears ran down my face. As I reached for it, the feather floated to me and stood in my hand. Then I heard a sudden noise, like an explosion, and all the blankets fell off the windows. I ran over to the nearest window and looked out. An eagle was flying away, as though it had broken right through the glass from our room.

Moments like these have confirmed for me that we are all connected, and the doors are opening wider between our time and all other times. We are here to turn the tide of time and the wisdom of the elders is available to help us. The golden thread of connection among all races is there, and feathers can bring us together in many ways. *The Earth is a perfect Mother*, if we will listen to her and learn from her. ❧

Hawk Music

Maril Crabtree

Feathers spread into fingers,
Hawk falls with the wind,
spiraling down as if caught
in a place of no hope—

a daredevil's pitch, "do or die,"

then lifting again, drifting
where hope and wind
take him, whistling, into
the strumming air, filled

with a cloudless lullaby.

Now listen as symphony's
sweeping sounds carve
themselves out of his flapping
wings, singing and swinging

across an arpeggio sky. 🦅

Guardian Hawk

Amy Belanger

IN 1990, I HAD THE PRIVILEGE TO SERVE AS an Ozark Mountains regional representative at the 1990 North American Bioregional Congress. This national gathering of Greens, environmental and ecological leaders, back-to-the-landers, and community dwellers came together to coordinate and expand our environmental protection efforts.

For three days, we communed at a summer camp in Maine, discussing how our alternative value system could positively impact the issues facing the world. Each morning, we rose by dawn to cook pancakes together in the camp kitchen, participate in yoga classes at the edge of the forest, or paddle a canoe through the deep mist atop the lake. All day we brought together the variant views of forest protection activists, urban environmentalists, animal rights advocates, and those defending poor communities from toxic waste sites.

Between sessions, we immersed ourselves in the forest we worked to protect, taking short hikes, splashing in the lake, and learning one another's unique understandings of the world. At night, the southerners among us played bluegrass music while others sang, danced, told stories, or wandered off to continue the debates of the day.

Often we gathered by the lake, sitting cross-legged in workshop circles, with the sunshine warming pine needles to a soft perfume, chipmunks scurrying for cover, and a regal hawk circling above, as if to say "I am watching over you."

By the last day, we knew that some deep personal change was required of those who wish to have a lasting impact on the world. We not only had to teach the world how to take care of the earth, but we also had to manifest the spiritual lessons of those who teach in the face of adversity. We had to learn to rework our language to reach those who didn't know what we did, heal our own despair in the face of daily reminders of what we were losing, and remain peaceful and compassionate against hostile opposition. By the last day, we each knew we had grown as teachers and joined one another as much in spirit as in mind.

On that cool spring day with the sky brightened by the sun and by the joy in our hearts, we assembled for our closing ceremony at the lakeside clearing. Two hundred world-changers held hands in a large circle, passing a hawk feather as a revival of the ancient Native American speaking stick, each one in turn blessing the events of the gathering. On the ground near the circle, someone spotted a feather. It was the feather of our guardian hawk, and we chose to accept it as a parting gift from a fellow traveler.

We bowed our heads to pray, meditate, and listen to the solemn words of wisdom spoken by our ceremony leader, who raised our talking feather to thank the guardian hawk who had graced our gathering all weekend. From time to time in our discussions we had seen it, crisscrossing the sky or hanging almost motionless in the clouds, and it had become a symbol, for us, of everything we were working for. It was one of those rare moments when the tender pressure of another's hands and the glowing of eyes meeting across the circle says, "we are one."

We raised our clasped hands and looked to the sky in our final moment of closure. Sighs of awe filled the circle as we witnessed our sacred sentinel, the guardian hawk, following the exact form of our circle just above us, completing the blessing with an unforgettable salute.

Meditation

A WALK IN THE WOODS

Breitenbush, a retreat center in Oregon, rests in the heart of the Cascades and is known for its natural hot mineral springs. But the most wondrous thing for me is the ancient forest that surrounds Breitenbush. Reading the orientation brochures, I learn that these are some of the oldest trees on the continent. I am disheartened to learn that less than 5 percent of America's original forest is intact today.

As I hike through the thickly populated cedars, redwoods, and birches, it is hard to imagine that these trees are an "endangered species." They are full of vitality, reaching hundreds of feet into the sky. Those that have fallen naturally have trunks more than eight feet wide. Some of the fallen trees span the river and have been planed flat, with log handrails attached, to provide safe crossings.

Then I hike on the perimeter of a section that has been logged and reseeded. The contrast is stunning. Here, the tallest trees are four feet. There is no shady woodland, only harsh sun and sparse undergrowth. It will take many decades for the forest to come even close to its former majesty.

I wonder what our land will look like when the last 5 percent is gone. The woman I am hiking with is a native of Oregon; she tells me that the logging industry now has permission to cut in national forests. These forests, formerly preserved, now are open to the loggers' saws at an alarming rate.

They cut down the trees to within a few feet of the highways going through the national parks, she says, so tourists are not aware of the extent of deforestation. We drive by tall woods that seem to go back from the road for miles; actually, the forest is only thirty feet deep before the trees are replaced by bare undergrowth and tiny seedlings.

I think of my feathers. What will happen when all the trees disappear? Already the songbirds are at risk in many areas, forced to find new habitats each time development encroaches on their tree-homes. Not only will we not have huge, ancient trees to view and be shaded by — we also won't have birds to see and hear, or other small creatures. And without birds, there will be no feathers to add their beauty to the world, no feathers to find on a forest path.

At that moment, as if to underscore my thoughts, a feather appears on the hiking trail. It speaks its warning: "Don't take me for granted. I may not be here for your grandchildren."

The signs of an endangered planet are all around us, even when we're only looking for feathers. Maybe that's why the universe seems to be sending its messages in every way it can, so we will know that the time to act — for our own future and for the future of generations to come — is now. The gift of feathers is also a message to protect and love all forms of life on the planet, so that its gifts will continue to be here for all.

* *Take a walk.* As in the Buddhist form of "walking meditation," walk slowly and deliberately enough to be aware of each step.
* *With each step,* name and give thanks for some part of the planet and all its varied inhabitants.
* *Be especially mindful* of any new steps you might take to help protect our earth for future generations, and ask for a blessing of your future movement in that direction.

Part Three

Light as a Feather:

Messages of Freedom,

Surrender, and Letting Go

Feathers and Grace

Maril Crabtree

ON A RECENT TRIP TO SAN FRANCISCO, MY airplane seatmate told me to visit Grace Cathedral. For the past several years, people have come from all over the world to this historic cathedral to participate in a spiritual experience known as "walking the labyrinth." The ancient pattern of an eleven-circuit labyrinth path, found embedded on the floor of Chartres Cathedral in France, was brought to San Francisco by Dr. Lauren Andress, an Episcopal priest, as a rediscovered tool for contemplation and reflection on one's spiritual life.

The moment I heard about the labyrinth, I knew I would go there. That afternoon, I headed over to Nob Hill and soon found the tall spires of the cathedral nestled among the city's renowned steep streets and colorful row houses.

When I walked up to the huge church, I noticed a little coffee shop called Cup of Grace in its street-level basement. I couldn't resist going in for a cup of San Francisco latte. The shop was inviting and cheerful, with a few tables by the window looking out on a small park across the street. Farther back were rows of books, shelves of religious paraphernalia, and CDs. Soft Gregorian chant music played in the background.

The shop manager obligingly chatted with me

about the labyrinth and regaled me with story after story of its power in people's lives. As I turned to go upstairs for my own labyrinth experience, I felt a small feather in my pocket. I had found it while walking around the zoo the weekend before. Instead of immediately putting it with my other feathers, though, for some reason I had kept it in the pocket of this jacket. Now I knew why. I pulled it out.

"I'd like to give you a small gift in return for all the things you've shared with me," I said, offering the manager my feather. I explained to him why feathers are special for me. He thanked me. "I'll put this on my altar at home and it will remind me to share myself with people," he said.

I was content. A gift well given and graciously received, especially with a stranger, has its own sacred quality in our busy world. The exchange of my feather for the experience of this man's sharing of time was a satisfying one.

The next day, having walked the indoor labyrinth with a dozen people who, like me, came to experience this unique form of contemplative prayer, I returned to walk the outdoor labyrinth. It had been carved in stone on a large courtyard area adjacent to the coffee shop. The manager had mentioned that the outdoor labyrinth was an entirely different experience, and so it was. A man doing tai chi in a far corner of the courtyard greeted me with a silent bow. He and I were the only humans embracing the crisp morning air here, along with a few pigeons that seemed to be content to create their own path.

After I completed my labyrinth walk, I decided to go to the coffee shop for another latte and one last thank-you to the manager. As I approached the shop and was about to enter, I glanced down. There, next to a small scarlet hibiscus bush, lay a beautiful white feather.

I knew immediately that it was for me. The universe, in that way it has of blessing us with abundance, had replaced the feather I'd given away with one that would give me a treasured memory of the special place it came from.

I held the feather in my hands and gave thanks for the mysterious, yet simple, ways in which the universe communicates. "Starting here, starting now," I thought, as I cradled the delicate white feather in my hands, "I'll look for more opportunities to give—to give my feathers *and* myself." Startled, I realized that I had affirmed the intention the manager had declared the day before, when he said that the feather I gave him would remind him to share himself with others.

The white feather is still with me. But I know that I'll find its next owner soon . . .

Giving Back

Terrill Petri

FOR THE PAST THREE YEARS, I HAVE BEEN collecting feathers. They seem to be there for me whenever I take a walk, wherever I go. Why? I'm not sure, but my daughter, who I consider to be a wise woman, says that feathers have to do with transitions, and with moving on to where you're meant to be.

In the past few years I have gone from having my own full-time public relations business to being director of Women Vision International, a non-profit organization that works with women of indigenous cultures in the United States, Africa, and South America. I use my business skills and knowledge to help other women around the world become empowered through starting their own businesses.

In the course of teaching empowerment, I've learned a lot from these women who live simple lives of survival, taking care of themselves and their children using whatever skills and talents they possess. They have few material comforts but are often rich in ways of appreciating the gifts of nature that are available to all of us. They seem to know that somehow their needs will be taken care of, with an assurance I've often envied as I struggle to raise funds for my organization.

This past spring, while working at the Pine Ridge Reservation with a group of Native American women, I pulled something from a stack of papers and a feather fell out. One of the women smiled and said, "It's a mourning dove feather. That will be your Native American name: Mourning Dove." Touched by this gift of both a feather and a name, I put the feather in my wallet, so that I would always have it with me.

A month later I traveled to Africa, again working with a group of indigenous women. One day we hiked to a section of Victoria Falls known as the Devil's Cauldron. Water surged and swirled hundreds of feet below the grassy cliff where we stood peering over the edge. One of the women told me that it was an ancient tradition to throw something into the water that you want to release. "I really want to let go of my fears and struggles," I thought. "Maybe here is the place."

I remembered my special mourning dove feather, and I also remembered the Native American tradition of "giving back." Whenever you receive a gift from the universe, it's important to give something back, as a way of saying thank you. I took the feather out of my wallet. It was time to give it back, and let it take my fears with it.

I threw my feather out toward the falls, expecting that it would fall short of the edge we stood on, and land on the grass in front of me. Instead, the wind caught it and floated it out over the edge. I watched as it dropped straight into the

Devil's Cauldron. At that instant, a beautiful black and white butterfly landed right at the spot where I had focused my attention: the butterfly, a universal symbol of transformation! In that moment I felt utter peace, knowing that my prayer for release of my fears had been heard.

Returning the feather to the universe was a good way to give thanks to Mother Earth for her care of me and to walk toward the future secure in the knowledge that I would continue to be taken care of. ✍

Angels at My Feet

Vicki Wagoner

I am a feather for each wind that blows.
—Shakespeare, *The Winter's Tale*,
Act II, Scene 3

I WORK IN A BUSY OFFICE BUILDING, SUR-
rounded by four lanes of traffic driving by in each
direction. Across the boulevard, however, lies a
lake where I like to sit, read, and meditate during
my lunch hour. The lake is small but serene, with
tall pines and flowering bushes bordering it.
Despite the traffic, I soon "tune out" and tune into
the beauty of the water, the clouds, and the wildlife
that come there. There are numerous birds, mostly
white egrets and ducks, an occasional great blue
heron, a few little fish, and often funny black water
birds that dive deep into the lake and emerge several yards away, shaking themselves vigorously.

One day as I was crossing the grass on the way
to my spot by the lake, I stopped dead in my tracks.
A few feet in front of me, nine white cattle egrets
and one great blue heron all stood motionless,
facing the same direction. I remembered seeing just
such a scene in the movie *City of Angels*. There, the
angels (in human form) gathered each morning at
sunrise on the beach to give thanks to their Creator

for another day. They all silently and solemnly faced the same direction. The scene had made an impact on me because it felt so serene, so sacred.

Now the egrets and heron were standing at attention in the same way and, it seemed to me, with the same deep serenity. I was frozen. It was the most amazing sight I have ever seen. They stayed that way for several minutes and finally, a few at a time, flew away.

I ate lunch, read, and meditated as usual. The day was sunny and beautiful, with fluffy white clouds, a comfortable breeze, and a magical atmosphere.

When I got up to return to work, I took a few steps and heard the message, "The gift is at your feet." I looked down. There on the ground were nine white feathers and one gray-blue feather.

I silently thanked the angels for visiting me. Their message was clear. With the challenges of a new full-time career, a second job to help make ends meet, a husband, and two teenage sons, I often feel overwhelmed and out of balance, despite my attempts to let go and trust that all will be well. I tend to keep myself trapped and weighed down by my own lack of faith. Yet again and again, angels have found ways of letting me know that I am loved, protected, and guided.

I collected the gift of feathers and put them in a cup on my desk. Imprinted on the cup are the words *Be Free*. Each time I glance at them, I remember the silent serenity of the birds—my angels in disguise—and their incredible gift. ✍

A Burden Light
as a Feather

Robert Gass, Ed.D.

THE CANYONLANDS WILDERNESS OF UTAH IS one of my places of vision and power. I go to the desert, with its primal sandstone turrets, obelisks, and spires and pristine beauty, for clarity and solitude.

I was on a ten-day solo retreat, staying in a remote cabin at a ranch that offered such spiritual haven. I spent the first days emptying myself of the stress and speed of modern daily life. As I became quiet, I put out prayers for guidance about direction in my work and life. In one of my meditations, I heard that I was to write a book on energy and work with individual leaders as a guide and coach.

The next day, I'd left the ranch to hike in a nearby canyon, and climbed partway up one of the red sandstone walls. I was feeling very agitated about my "assignment" and spontaneously started talking out loud to God.

"Okay, God, what about this book and this work? You know, I don't need to do this stuff anymore. I really get that I don't need to do important things in the world to be happy; in fact, I'd be quite happy doing very little for the next while. If this is important and serves you, I'll do it. Otherwise, I don't know. Please give me some kind of sign if this really matters to you. Some kind of physical sign so that I'll know this is really mine to do."

All of a sudden, it started raining. Concerned about the rock becoming slippery, I descended rapidly, forgot about the conversation, the sign, and God, and started walking back to the ranch. About fifteen minutes later, I turned around. There was a rainbow. One end went directly into the rock I had been standing on.

Rather than finding this reassuring, I became far more agitated. "That's a sign. Definitely a sign . . . Well, maybe not. Rainbows do happen . . . But that's the promise God gave to Moses. It's the classic sign of the covenant of God and man . . . So now you think you're Moses? Sign, *schmine*, it's a rainbow."

I debated the point all the way to my cabin.

Beginning to feel desperate, I talked to God again.

"Okay, I know this is asking a lot. I asked for a sign, and there was a rainbow coming right out of the rock where I stood. I should be feeling grateful, but I feel scared and confused. I have doubt. Maybe doubt isn't handled by signs. But if it serves, I would ask for one more sign. A sign so clear and unmistakable that even my doubting fears will be stilled. I ask that a feather come to me in some unmistakably magical way. I also understand that I may not get this sign. Maybe I need to live with doubt, and that's okay."

At that point, I released it. I felt a letting-go inside. Even if the sign did not come, I was prepared to accept my assignment as best I understood it.

That morning, a group of women had come to the ranch for a ceremony. They had heard from the ranch owner that I was in the retreat cabin. My musical recordings were an important part of their group life, and they sent a delegation to ask if I might be willing to come and sing a few songs at their ceremonial fire that evening.

I suppose I should have felt honored, but I was a little grumpy. *I'm supposed to be on retreat,* I thought to myself. I was going to say no, but I remembered my request to God. I felt, in this moment, that that spirit was in the form of these women, and I smiled and accepted.

That evening, we gathered around the fire for prayers, songs, and dancing. The evening was finished. I was packing up my guitar when a woman stepped up to me. She looked me in the eye and said, "Here, this is for you. I heard I was supposed to give it to you." In her hand was the feather of a red-tailed hawk.

As my hand touched the feather, I heard the voice of my doubting self try to come up with a counterargument. And there was none. For once, my inner skeptic was speechless.

The feather sits on my altar as a reminder of God's will. ✍

Magpie Feather
Paul W. Anderson, Ph.D.

DESPITE THE 175,399 MILES ON MY OLD DODGE van, it toiled faithfully through the night under a sky that looked like sequins sewn onto black velvet. Alternating driving and sleeping, my wife, Pam, and I held on while the van chewed up the long flat miles between Kansas City and Taos, New Mexico.

As the sun climbed up the eastern side of the Sangre de Cristo Mountains and surprised the sage-covered mesa into another day, we ate breakfast burritos and red chilies at our favorite restaurant. That one meal was worth the thirteen-hour trip.

By noon I had finished several errands, and we were ready for our room at the Old Taos Guest House. Barefoot Tim, one of the owners, met us in the gravel parking lot. In the manner typical of the slower pace of Taos, he gave us a brief history and tour of the 100-year-old hacienda. The pink adobe walls, wide veranda, blooming hollyhocks, and big-sky view of the western mesa left me feeling at home, right where I needed to be. Tim's last instruction was how to use the hot tub just outside our room.

With a towel draped over my shoulders, I pre-ceded Pam to the tub. As I explored the sur-rounding area, I stopped near a setting of two chairs and a small table. Behind one of the chairs, near the bushes, was a black-and-white magpie feather. Long blades of grass held it suspended above the earth as if offering it to me, saying, "Here, take the feather you asked for. It's yours. The birds left it for you."

Synchronicity is like a psychic sneeze for me. Things get reset. I catch up with myself and once again know I'm in the right place at the right time. I stood there with my mouth agape and received the feather I forgot I had asked for three months earlier. And although the outer event of finding that feather coincided with my inner experience in an emotionally meaningful and symbolic way, the full impact and teaching of this feather was yet to come.

Feathers come into my life as powerful symbols of various kinds of energies but usually unexpectedly. Bending over to pick up the feather, I remembered that the time I had asked for a feather was three months ago, in March, when Pam and I had been in Taos to celebrate our wedding anniversary.

Magpies remind me of the black-and-white-striped kachina clowns in the Zuni tradition. These birds are the tricksters, the coyotes of the bird kingdom with friendly vocalizations that tease me into being caught off-guard. They run in gangs, mate for life, and, like their crow relatives, fill the space around themselves with audacious power.

I had wanted some of that energy, and in March, I had asked every magpie I saw for a symbolic donation of its power. At first, I wanted a long tail feather, solid black with a purple sheen. As the March days wore on and no feather was forthcoming, I told the birds I'd be happy to accept anything. The magpies seemed to laugh at me. Mostly, I felt ignored, my request for one of their feathers discounted. I returned to Kansas City empty-handed. Magpie feathers did not occur to me again until now, when this one appeared.

After thanksgiving and cleansing rituals, I attached the feather to a new flute I had bought. Throughout the weekend, I played the flute for magpies when they came near me. As usual they ignored me and my music, but they did seem happy with the early summer green that replaced the winter brown, and the puffs of white cloud that floated through the vast sky.

Sunday was the day to return home. It was also Solstice. I rose early so I could be at the Rio Grande gorge for sunrise before we left. I wanted to pray and honor the day at a spot where last year I had watched a red-tailed hawk hatch two young birds. Perhaps she'd be there again.

In the early-morning light, I took my drum and flute with the new magpie feather, unlocked the van, and put the key in the ignition. I turned the key to crank the engine and get going. Nothing happened. The key would not budge. The ignition switch was frozen. I tried everything I knew to get the van started. Stuck, stuck, stuck.

By now, I had given up on going to the gorge and was worried about getting home. Tim was in the kitchen baking muffins and cutting up fruit for breakfast. He suggested I call the one guy in the phone book advertised as a twenty-four-hour emergency locksmith.

"Hi, I'm sorry to bother you like this on a Sunday, but I can't turn the key in the ignition and I need to get my van started so I can get back to Kansas City today. Can you help me?"

"Ah, man, this is early. You say Kansas City?"

"Yeah, Kansas City. We're over here at the Old Taos Guest House."

"Ah, how 'bout you call me back in a couple of hours and I can tell you then when I can get out there." Click.

I went back to Tim. "Got any graphite? Maybe that'll loosen up something."

"Yeah, I do. It's out in the shed."

"I'll get it. Just tell me where it is."

"No, you wait here. I'll get it for you." Tim wiped banana and citrus juice off his hands and drifted to the shed.

I waited, finally got the graphite and shot some into the ignition switch. No luck. Three years earlier, the van had been stolen. The thieves had broken something on the steering column and hot-wired the ignition. Maybe I could do the same thing. But I didn't want to break anything, and anyway, I wasn't sure what to break. Another plan was to take the steering wheel off and, I hoped, expose the ignition wires that way. I went back to Tim.

"Got any sockets?" I explained my plan to him.

"Yeah," he said. "Out in the shed."

"Want me to go get them?" I asked.

"No. Wait here and I'll get them for you."

I stood there on the stoop looking at a new day expanding west across the vast mesa. "I hate to wait," I said to myself. Then the *a-ha* hit me. That's what this was about. That was the message. "Wait!"

The sockets didn't work. By now, Pam had come out to see what was going on. I told her the scenario. "This is all about waiting," I told her. "I hate to wait. I had to wait for the magpie feather, the locksmith, the graphite, the sockets, and my trip to the gorge. I don't like to wait."

As I spoke, I put the key in the ignition once more. I turned the key and the van started.

Pam laughed. "I think you got the message," she said. The ignition has worked fine ever since.

We packed the van, drove out of the gravel parking lot, and headed for the street. Fifty feet from the blacktop, a big magpie flew in front of the van, landed, and proceeded to strut slowly ahead of us. He acted like the drum major in front of a parade band.

We followed as the bird reached the road and turned left, the direction we needed to go. He chattered and rattled at us the whole time. Soon he stopped walking and, without effort, floated to the bottom wire of the barbed wire fence along the side of the road.

The magpie sat there silently. I leaned out the window. "Thanks for the feather," I said. "I think I got the message." He flung another squawk at me. In slow motion, he opened his black-and-white wings, fanned out his long black tail, and glided off into the distant field. ✑

Meditation

Gifts and Signs from Feathers

Feathers from certain birds have long been known to symbolize specific signs or omens in many ancient cultures. These signs have permeated our language: wise as an owl, the bluebird of happiness, swift as an eagle. Although a feather can have a specific message that is individual to each person, there are universal messages we can learn from as well:

- **Crow, raven** — intuitive knowledge, mystical wisdom (The raven is also seen as a messenger of death or illness in some traditions. Edgar Allen Poe's *The Raven* speaks to both the mystery and ill-omened nature of the bird.)
- **Eagle, hawk** — swiftness, strength, courage; associated with masculine energy, the yang principle, sacred birds in many cultures, often seen as "messenger" birds
- **Kingfisher** — happiness, prosperity, good fortune
- **Owl** — inner wisdom, associated with feminine energy, the yin principle
- **Peacock** — a symbol of protection or clairvoyant vision; also a symbol of love and sensual joy
- **Pigeon** — adaptation and survival
- **Rainbow Bird** — a mythical bird that comes from exotic rainforest lore, bringing happiness and prosperity to those who glimpse it among the dense foliage
- **Robin** — a messenger of good weather if seen chirping on an open branch, and rain if hidden in a tree; also represents innocence and "good luck."
- **Rook** — another harbinger of good weather if seen high in a tree, rainy weather if low; many perching together indicate a storm is on its way
- **Seagulls** — peace, eternity
- **Stork** — good fortune, many children

For this meditation, set aside a day, a weekend, or a week. Declare an intention to notice what birds come into your view. Jot down the types of birds you notice. Look up their potential meanings in several sources, such as David Carson's Medicine Cards, books on bird lore, or a good dictionary with historical and literary annotations.

When you have gathered all the meanings, find a quiet place to meditate. Ask your inner wisdom what meanings could be applied to your life at that moment. Allow some time for the answers to emerge. Write down whatever is given to you. Ask for continuing guidance from the world of nature, and especially from feathers.

Black Bird, White Bird

Laura Giess

WHEN I FIRST SAW THE BIRDS, I WAS STILL married and living in a tiny western Kansas town. I had found a job in Hays, sixty miles away, and commuted each day, the first thirty miles along a two-lane highway, then another thirty miles of four-lane freeway.

My marriage had increasingly deteriorated, and I was in despair about what to do. Should I keep trying, or should I move out and hope that the process of separation would bring clarity? These thoughts constantly seesawed in my head, but I couldn't seem to find an answer.

One morning while I was driving to work, a white bird and a black bird flew up out of a wheat field and passed directly over my Explorer. They came out of nowhere, just the two of them; and the stark contrast of their colors startled me into awareness. Although I usually notice birds, I had not noticed such an unlikely pair flying together before.

"I wonder who is trying to communicate with me," I thought as I watched the birds fly across my field of vision. I tried to get a sense of someone, but no one came to mind, so I let it go.

But the next day, it happened again, in the

same way and in the very same place—one black bird and one white flying together up out of this field and heading right over the top of my vehicle. It wasn't as though I was scaring them up out of the grass; there was no logical explanation for their behavior.

Nevertheless, on most days I drove to work, wrestling with whether to move out and start over, as I passed the field, I saw the birds fly up: always two birds, one black and one white, and always in the same place. I always thought, "Who *is* this? What are they trying to tell me?"

Gradually, I realized that the birds seemed to be a symbol of my inner emotions, and the conflict that I felt: part black and part white. My life was in turmoil. Finally, after a month of deliberating, I made up my mind. With great difficulty, I told my husband and my two teenage boys that I needed to move out and seek some solution for my increasing unhappiness. I found a small apartment not far from work and, with fear and determination, moved in and began a new life.

After I moved to Hays, I saw the white bird again several times, but I never saw the black one again. When I finally made a choice to start a new life, I knew in my heart that I had made the right decision, no matter how painful the consequences would be. The disappearance of the black bird, and the continued appearances of the white one, seemed to confirm my choice. Now that I'm happy, relaxed, and free, I see white birds often! ✑

Feather Hunt

Mark E. Tannenbaum

A feather in hand is better than a bird in the air.
—George Herbert, *Jacula Prudentum*

IN GENERAL, PEOPLE ARE COLLECTORS. I know people who collect Beanie Babies, Barbie Dolls, and baseball cards. At one time in my life I collected bottle caps; later I graduated to beer cans and bottles. There really was no reason for me to collect bottle caps or beverage containers; it just seemed to express the hunter-gatherer part of me.

When my life was in crisis, I discovered that the collector instinct was again opening—not like the previous time, but into something more powerful. I can only relate this to a whisper I remember hearing when my twin brother slid past me in my mother's womb: "Enjoy the journey." It was a faint whisper on the wind similar to a bird that hovers over you; then, in a quick beat of its wings, that whisper is there. It is profound.

It was a powerful time in my life. So many voices of nature were coming my way that I thought I would have to wear earplugs to silence them! Everything blossomed as if azalea buds were blooming in my eyes. Intoxicating fragrances and new feelings surrounded me, caressing my mind, spirit, and body. I was beginning again. Another hunter-gatherer phase? Not in the sense of what I was, but in whom I was to become.

What took me to the next phase was *Animal Speak*, a book written by Ted Andrews that explained how the things of nature have their own significance. I became more aware of what surrounded me. Simply put, it was a balance that I was seeking.

Through my reading, I found that my awareness of nature expressed itself especially with birds. They were my totem family. I felt more aligned than ever but still lacked the key to open the door of direct experience.

On a long weekend in mid-September, I took *Animal Speak*, my dog, Yapper, and my camping gear and drove to Shades State Park in Indiana to look for "the key" that Ted Andrews wrote about. I wondered what it would take to find it. If it was in this area, I had over 2,000 acres to cover in three days!

On the morning of the third day, I started walking with Yapper, following no marked trail. By this time I had convinced myself that there was no real urgency to find the key. Since this was my last day—and since I had nothing to lose—I asked for the key out loud.

"I want to find a feather, preferably a red-tailed hawk feather," I spoke into the woods. Then I forgot about the whole thing. I nonchalantly kept walking, following Yapper since she seemed to know where to go.

After a while, a shadow came over me. It felt as if someone were tapping me on the shoulder, whispering again in my ear, "Enjoy the journey." Even Yapper noticed the shadow and began to bark at it.

I glanced up at the sky. There they were—two red-tailed hawks in flight! I was stunned. I paused, thanked Father Sky and Mother Earth for the gift, and followed them along the path as they flew. When we finally came to a clearing, Yapper and I were both gasping for air.

I saw some wooden benches in a circle in the clearing. I noticed something on a bench and walked over to it. A feather stood upright between the bench slats, placed there for me. I picked it up and felt both its fragility and its inner magnificence. It was a true moment of wonder: a key, an access to doorways at a level I had never experienced, a new balance created in my life.

Since then, I have found many feathers. They are not only gifts from nature; they are also a symbol of life renewing itself. Each time a feather falls, another feather takes its place. This new life from old life reminds me that death is only a beginning: where there is death, there is life, a balance.

And along the way, I remember what the red-tailed hawk whispered in my ear: "Enjoy the journey." ✍

A Spirit of Freedom

Terry Podgornik

ABOUT TWO YEARS AGO, A FEATHER CROSSED my path. I noticed it. It seemed important somehow, but I wasn't quite sure what to make of it.

Since then, feathers have appeared often, almost out of nowhere. Most curious of all, even when I find myself in urban surroundings with no birds in sight, feathers make their way into my life. Sometimes, as I leave work, in the midst of a tangle of tall buildings, speeding cars, and busy pedestrians, a feather floats down and falls right in front of my feet.

Feathers give me a connection to something beyond myself and my usual worries. When I took a trip to Scotland, I spent lots of time touring all the must-see sights and buying gifts. As I was standing in a little shop trying to decide which scarf to buy, I looked up and saw a young man with hawk feathers in his hair. We were strangers, but we smiled at each other across the store. In that instant, we shared a secret companionship, connected by the feathers. I left feeling refreshed, despite the weary hours I'd spent as a tourist traveling from store to store.

I've finally understood that feathers represent spiritual freedom to me. They encourage me to focus on what's really important in life. They remind me to take the time to renew myself, to enjoy life, to live in the present moment. It's a simple but powerful message, one that I need to hear often.

I've decided that, if feathers can make their way to me even in the middle of a city, I owe it to them and to myself to make my way out of the city to more natural surroundings, where the reminder to enjoy life and appreciate nature surrounds me constantly.

I have feathers to thank for taking more time for personal retreats, long walks in parks and along rivers, and vacations in wildlife areas. With the appearance of each new feather, I grow stronger in listening to my inner wisdom. ✍

One Heart

Li-Young Lee

Look at the birds. Even flying
is born

out of nothing. The first sky
is inside you, Friend, open

at either end of day.
The work of wings

was always freedom, fastening
one heart to every falling thing.

You Don't Have to Struggle

Lee Lessard-Tapager

LIKE MANY PEOPLE, THE STATE OF MY OWN health became an avenue for switching careers and doing something I love. I had a troublesome knee injury that refused to get better with traditional treatment. I explored alternatives and eventually attained healing through holistic kinesiology and working with "stuck" places in my energy patterns. Now I teach holistic health and healing to a wide variety of people.

Shortly after taking the bold step of quitting my former job and deciding to teach what I had learned through my own recovery, I began to collect feathers. I wanted to create a healing space for my work that would include sacred objects from nature.

Once I had the intention to use feathers in my space, they came across my path more and more frequently. I took long walks on Pine Island (off the Gulf coast of Florida), where my yoga teaching and healing practice were beginning to take shape. It was one of those periods when nothing seemed to come easily—everything was a struggle, and I worked constantly to establish a stable financial base for my new venture.

One day I was walking along, wondering why

everything seemed to take so much effort, when I saw a beautiful white feather perched in a marshy field beside the road. The only problem was that it was surrounded by water. I wanted the feather, but I didn't want to wade through mud and water to get to it. I thought, "If I'm meant to have a feather like that, there will be another one for me sooner or later."

I walked around the next corner and was startled to see a huge flock of white ibis just taking off into the morning sun. As the flock passed overhead, a single white feather drifted down onto the path immediately in front of me.

The message was instantaneous and clear. "You don't have to struggle. Accept fully that the universe will provide what you need, when you need it."

That message was exactly what I needed to hear. Since then, whenever I have felt myself not accepting the timing of the universe, I look at the white ibis feather that was given to me that day. It reminds me that everything happens as it needs to.

Ritual

ABUNDANT FEATHERS, ABUNDANT LIVES

Choose a feather that calls to you, or choose an imaginary feather of your liking, and go to your favorite meditation spot.

* Place the feather in front of you on a rug, table, or altar space (or in your mind's eye if the feather is imaginary), and focus your energy into the feather-space.

* With your eyes open or closed, spend some quiet time with the feather, meditating on your strengths and positive qualities. Write them down either at the end of your meditating time or as you go along.

* Next, think of the places of love, comfort, and power in your life. What good friends are you blessed with? Where do you experience the feeling of inner power? What material blessings do you have? (Don't minimize here—remember, for the homeless, shelter is a great blessing; for the hungry, food on the shelves for the next meal is a definite plus!) If you wish, draw or sketch these places of comfort and power.

* Hold the feather in your hand. Starting at the crown of your head, slowly draw it down one side of your body, then the other, then in front of you and behind you. Make a "field" of feather energy that surrounds your body. As you do, speak (out loud if you can) the words "I am blessed with . . ." followed by the things you have thought of, written down, and sketched. Here are some examples:

    * I am blessed with intelligence.
    * I am blessed with a sense of humor.
    * I am blessed with an appreciation for life itself.
    * I am blessed with a comfortable bed, lots of good books, and enough money to meet my needs.

- I am blessed with friends who care for me enough to be honest with me and to accept me.
- I am blessed with a beautiful garden in my back-yard where I feel my own power and the power of nature.

Don't worry if you run out of specifics. Keep saying the words, "I am blessed" as you create the feather-field. As you do so, you will continue to attune yourself to the universal field of positive energy that surrounds us all the time. 🪶

Fifty Things to Do with Feathers

Mary-Lane Kamberg

FOR MY FIFTIETH BIRTHDAY, A FRIEND SENT me fifty feathers. My thank-you note to her was this list of fifty things to do with feathers:

1. Feather my nest.
2. Put a feather in my cap.
3. Tickle myself pink.
4. Flock together with birds of the same feather.
5. Tar and feather someone.
6. Write with a quill pen.
7. Place a quill pen and inkwell next to your computer to remind yourself how far communications have come.
8. Sleep on a feather bed.
9. Sleep on a feather pillow.
10. Dust with a feather duster.
11. Decide which weighs more: a pound of feathers or a pound of iron.
12. Make a Christmas wreath.
13. Cover up with a down comforter.
14. Wear a down ski jacket.
15. Tickle my fancy.

16. Tickle my husband's nose while he's asleep.
17. Tickle a baby's toes.
18. Make an Indian headdress.
19. Join the Quill and Scroll Journalism Society.
20. Make angel wings.
21. Make a Big Bird costume.
22. Make a dream catcher.
23. Make a Mardi Gras mask.
24. Make my cat think there's a bird nearby.
25. Hold a feather in my trunk, flap my ears, and learn to fly.
26. Feather my bangs.
27. Shoot an arrow.
28. Wear a boa.
29. Cover myself with a *Ziegfeld Follies* fan.
30. Leave a feather on the ground where a child can find it.
31. Feel I'm in fine feather.
32. Use a nom de plume.
33. Pity the plumage, but forget the dying bird.
34. Pretend I'm a plumed knight.
35. Make hats for a marching band.
36. Signal the Huguenots.
37. Preen.
38. Smooth someone's feathers.
39. Ruffle someone's feathers.
40. Make a ruff for a female sandpiper.

41. Embroider with a featherstitch.
42. Box with someone who weighs between 118 and 127 pounds.
43. Strengthen something with a wedge.
44. Turn the blade of an oar so it is horizontal to the surface of the water.
45. Make a wake with a submarine periscope.
46. Use a featherbone for a corset stay.
47. Connect a tongue and groove joint.
48. Call someone a featherbrain.
49. Identify a flaw in a gemstone.
50. Hire more employees than necessary, pursuant to union rules. ✑

What's Your Feather Factor?

Virginia Lore

CAN YOU SPEAK WITH THE ANGELS OR FLY like an eagle? Find out what message the feather has for you in this quick quiz.

1. Your first conscious act in the morning is to:
   A. Meditate for a few minutes
   B. Order up a tall double mocha with extra whipped cream
   C. Turn to the editorial page in the newspaper
   D. Wake up the kids on your way to the kitchen

2. Walking through a parking lot, you notice:
   A. The fresh smell of rain on the asphalt
   B. The ice cream shop in the next block
   C. The gas-guzzling SUV illegally parked in a disabled space
   D. Which cars have infant seats

3. Your ideal vacation would be spent:
   A. At a retreat center
   B. On a luxury cruise liner
   C. Chained to a tree
   D. Visiting family and friends

4. If your TV is on, you're watching:
   A. The Wisdom Channel
   B. *Sex in the City*
   C. *Headline News*
   D. *The Waltons*

5. You frequently dream about:
   A. Flying
   B. Kissing
   C. Fighting
   D. Fleeing

6. In high school you could be found:
   A. Looking at clouds from the rooftop
   B. Making out backstage during play rehearsal
   C. Defending your underground newspaper in the vice principal's office
   D. Seeking respite in a bathroom stall

7. If you read more poetry, you'd start with:
   A. The metaphysical imagery of William Blake
   B. The rich syntax of Walt Whitman
   C. The naked truth of Lucille Clifton
   D. The simple domesticity of Emily Dickinson

8. You spend a lot of time at your computer:
   A. Doing automatic writing in your word processing program
   B. Playing games on the Web
   C. Sending political action e-mail
   D. Balancing your family's finances

9. On a hot Saturday afternoon, you are:
   A. In a Japanese garden, listening to a fountain
   B. In an air-conditioned movie theater, laughing at the latest comedy
   C. On a picket line, showing your support for the workers
   D. At a home improvement store, looking at fans

10. You would prefer to live:
    A. In the Boulder, Colorado, of the 1970s
    B. In the New York City of the Roaring '20s
    C. In the Washington, D.C. of the 1960s
    D. In the Kansas City of the 1950s

Scoring:

* *Mostly As: Angel Seeker.* Associated with the element of air, the Angel Seeker's primary realm is spirituality. Remarkably intuitive and very creative, Angel Seekers already have a strong relationship with the unseen and are highly receptive to messages from beyond. Remember the old saying, however: "Don't be so spiritual that you're no earthly good." The downfall of Angel Seekers is spiritual greed. Their challenge is to stay grounded enough to give their vision a practical focus. The feather's message is a reminder of the power on this plane, and the opportunity to connect to your physical circumstances.

* *Mostly Bs: Fan Dancer.* An ally of fire, the Fan Dancer's primary instinct is sensuality. In its shadow aspect, this can appear to be materialism or an attachment to carnality. This is the person most likely to have been a fan dancer in real life, or at least to have dabbled with the entertainment business. Healthy Fan Dancers, however, have harnessed the opportunity to practice joy in the physical world. Fan Dancers experience a sincere gratitude and enthusiasm for what other people would see as small experiences. The challenge for a Fan Dancer is to detach from the material details of daily life. When you find a feather, let it advise you to "be still and listen," or turn inward for a few moments of reflection before going about your busy life.

* *Mostly Cs: Eagle Speaker.* Partnered with the element of earth, the Eagle Speaker walks a journey of truth and justice. The Eagle Speaker's primary instinct is social, particularly in application to the greater good of all peoples. With their eyes always on the distant horizon, Eagle Speakers are not always skilled in one-on-one relationships and tend to be critical of anything (or anyone) falling short of their ideals. They are ruled by their passion for equity and can be critical of anything failing their ideals. Feathers cross the paths of Eagle Speakers to remind them of the joy to be found in the here-and-now when they release their judgments.

* *Mostly Ds: Safe Nester.* The Safe Nester's primary instinct is self-preservation in all of its manifestations. Ruled by water, Safe Nesters put enormous energy into strengthening their relationships and building their homes. A Safe Nester is not only likely to be a skilled gardener, cook, and parent but is also a great friend. Gifted with empathy and a heightened sensitivity, Safe Nesters can easily become morose, moody, or depressed. The feather prompts the Safe Nester to focus a little more energy on personal growth and to practice trust in an abundant universe.

Mixed Results:

* A *compatible pair* is a strong and healthy balance between two types (four or more answers in each category). For results, read both descriptions and allow the feather to carry both messages for you.
* An even split among three types (three in each) indicates a strong balance among three already developed sides of your personality. For growth, read the description of the type you scored the lowest on and let the feather help you develop the qualities of that aspect.
* An *absolute mix* (two to three in each of the four types) suggests that you are an individualist with a strong sense of your own worth and a unique set of tastes and values. While acknowledging that, allow the feather's message to inspire you to share your uniqueness by empowering others. ✍

Hawk Dreams

Judith Christy

I FIRST SAW HER IN MY DREAMS — A SHADOWY, mysterious presence. Then she began coming to me on the physical plane, and I knew I should pay attention to what she was showing me.

I was vacationing on an island off the Florida Gulf Coast. One day, a small hawk winged over my head and landed in a tree close to the house. Her coloring was beautiful, and I marveled at the detail of her feathers. I watched, fascinated, as she sat in the tree, and it seemed as if she returned my attention, matching look for look. Over the next few days, I saw her several more times.

One day I went out on the second-story deck to meditate in the sun. I sat in silence, eyes closed, letting thoughts go and emptying my mind. I was deeply into the dream state when I was startled by a fierce bird cry, a shadow passing over me, and something being dropped onto my lap. I opened my eyes to find a small branch with berries on it lying on my lap — my gift from the hawk. I was overwhelmed with this sacred connection.

Over the course of my two-week stay, she appeared almost daily, several times landing on the deck rail outside the kitchen door. I watched her through the screen door and even took her picture, which remains on my personal altar.

This lovely Florida red-shouldered hawk, a smaller and paler form of the red-shouldered hawk, became a symbol of freedom for me—a freedom that allows flight and exploration and takes new risks but always remains connected to the earth for sustenance and sanctuary. ✍

My Freedom Fan

Elissa Al-Chokhachy

In a corner of my bedroom is my altar and meditation stool. It is my place of retreat to experience inner silence and my sacred connection to Source. Upon my white altar cloth lay my most significant memoirs of my conscious spiritual journey. Pictures of enlightened beings, mystics, and prophets, such as the Blessed Mother, Gurumayi, Christ Jesus, and Sai Baba, offer me hope, especially in times of need.

One important treasure that resides on my altar is my "freedom fan," a bundle of various feathers that I have collected along the road to freedom. In March 1987, I had a profound spiritual awakening. Not only was I blessed with heightened awareness, I experienced the oneness of God in all things for several days. No longer was God out there or separate from me. I knew first-hand that God was *in me and in all things*. This realization transformed my life.

As a result, I committed myself fully to the spiritual path. It was truly a peak life experience. Ironically, along with the magnificent new awareness came the realization that my outer world did not support my new inner spiritual unfolding.

The years that followed were tumultuous, and my marriage of eighteen years ended in divorce. I prayed often for strength, courage, help, and healing. Amazingly, the universe responded with signs of hope and comfort.

I can't remember the actual day that the first feather of freedom appeared in my path. The fan and collection of feathers just naturally evolved on their own. Early in my spiritual journey, I attended an intense healing workshop. Afterward, a participant whom I had never met offered me a gift. It was something that he had kept for years; yet, inexplicably, he felt called to pass it on to me.

It was a rolled-up piece of sacred Indian cloth in earth tones, tied together with a leather string. Knowing it was special to him, I gratefully accepted his gift and felt moved by his generosity. Once home, I reverently placed it on my altar and gave thanks.

Around the same time, I was taking frequent reflective walks in order to center and balance myself. On a regular basis and especially in times of need, a feather would magically appear in my path. It didn't matter where I was. I could be in the woods, on the beach, or standing in a parking lot. I would find myself drawn to look in a certain direction, and there would be a feather lying on the ground beckoning to me. I would smile, knowing that it was a gift from Spirit.

Each feather was a milepost and a symbol that I was well on my way to freedom. I would pick up the feather and give thanks. When I got back to my altar, I would tuck the feather inside the leather tie of my Indian bundle. I had named the bundle my "freedom fan" because each feather represented one more step toward independence, wholeness, and autonomy . . . and one day, I knew that I would fly free.

Eight years from the time of my awakening, I was set free from my marriage. No longer did I have to pretend to be someone else's image of what I should be. I didn't have to hide my spirituality in a closet. I could breathe easily. I was finally free to be me.

Although I've struggled on my own as a single mother of three teens, my healing has continued, and I am now happier and freer than ever. My spirituality is incorporated into my work as a hospice nurse, and I am blessed with the most wonderful group of spiritual friends. They have supported me through the highs and lows of my journey.

The feathers come only occasionally now. But what is extraordinary is that, without even realizing it, I designed my new business card with a feather on it. Inspired by my youngest hospice patient ever, a fourteen-month-old child, I wrote an illustrated children's book, a heartwarming story about a special little angel who comes to earth for a short while and brings a gift of healing. Surely, he was an angel with feathered wings. Once again, the feathers in my path, this time of a heavenly nature, have helped me along my journey to personal freedom. ✍

The Unbearable Lightness of Feathers

Deborah Shouse

WHEN I WAS A CHILD, I LOVED BIRDS, AND I had a special love for feathers. I loved looking down and finding something beautiful, a bright blue symmetrical surprise among the dingy summer grasses. When I read the children's book, *The Flicker's Feather*, I began a search for such a magical feather that would bring good luck, as the story related.

I had seen flickers, but never experienced one of their feathers. One wretchedly hot summer day, I was with some other kids, playing a game of tag and about to get caught, when I saw my first flicker's feather. I stopped to pick it up, not caring that I was tagged and instantly dubbed IT. The hint of gold, the mystical connotations of that feather, transported me. Thus began my feather collection.

I kept the collection in a white Julius Lewis gift box. Julius Lewis was a fancy Memphis department store, and where my family got such a box, I don't know—unless maybe they had a radical markdown sale and my mother went dress shopping.

Every so often, an exotic feather appeared for my collection: a peacock feather caught in a bush at the zoo, flamingo feathers from a Florida trip, a hawk feather embedded in field stubble. I didn't much like people bringing me feathers; I wanted to be the finder. And I never took feathers from dead birds—that seemed like cheating.

I still have my collection. I like the feel of my feathers, the contrast of the soft plume and the sharp point. I like the colors and the combination of cunning camouflage and bright boldness.

But what I like most about my feathers is their lightness. I have a battered white box brimming with blue jay, mockingbird, cardinal, grackle, and seagull feathers, and the box still feels as though it's empty. Only when I take off the lid and open it up do I experience the magic and surprise of the treasures within. &

Meditation

FEATHER FANTASIES

Feathers can give you a feeling of the unknown, the exotic, the mysterious. Their delicate touch can send shivers through your body and send your senses soaring.

Spend some time thinking about feather fantasies. What have you always dreamed of doing—or having done to you—with feathers?

Find a quiet time and space for this meditation. As you read each idea, close your eyes and see the images that come to you. Take note of the feelings that accompany the images.

After you've moved through all of the ideas, return to your favorites and transform them into reality!

Sample fantasies:

* Perhaps you've always wanted your own huge feather fan, the kind the *Ziegfeld Follies* girls wore.
* Picture yourself lying in a bed completely covered with feathers . . . or picture them falling and covering you one by one as you lie there, eyes closed, feeling each feather as it falls.
* Wear a feather mask. You can buy them around Mardi Gras or Halloween—or make your own.
* Dress up in feathers: drape boas around your neck, wear satin dressing gowns trimmed with feathers. Complete the ensemble with feather earrings, hair barrettes, or a feather-trimmed hat.
* Hang feathers from your ceiling at various heights, some of which are at body level. Or make a feather mobile. The slightest breeze will set them moving, wafting through the air.
* With a partner or alone, try a feather massage. Use peacock or ostrich feathers, or any soft downy feathers. Try various touches: soothing, sensuous, stimulating . . .

Invitation

Kenneth Ray Stubbs, Ph.D.

A candle flame radiating

A finger resting

A peacock feather caressing

A mango melting

A stream of warm water searching

Arms embracing

Becoming One ✌

Wings of Freedom

Nancy Gifford ("Mumtaz")

AS AN ARTIST, I BEGAN COLLECTING FEATHERS and bird wings several years ago to incorporate into mixed-media assemblages. They spoke powerfully to me of freedom—every aspect of freedom, from political and social freedoms to freedom of the spirit.

For example, I have an assemblage called "Peace" containing an antique prosthetic hand from World War I. Its spring-loaded fingers hold one solitary gull peace feather.

An elderly collector purchased another assemblage called "Freeing of the Spirit." Later she called to tell me she had had a serious heart attack and was failing. She had hung the large construction on the wall opposite the foot of her bed so she could always see it.

"The wings are there to carry my spirit to the other side, " she said.

Her daughter called several weeks later to say her mother had passed on and confirmed how much the piece had comforted her in her last days. When she woke each morning, her daughter related, the first thing she would say was, "Oh, my wings haven't flown yet!"

Feathers and wings seem to come to me when I need them. On my honeymoon in Hawaii I admired the egrets that rode on the backs of the grazing cattle. They were beautiful, but I didn't want their wings because it would mean one of those elegant creatures would have to die.

The next day as we drove through the hills, an egret flew right into our windshield and was killed instantly. I felt compelled to honor it and still have photographs of me by the side of the road cutting off the wings. I always carry a pair of clippers with me. I feel somehow that birds have blessed me with their wings so they can be used in this way rather than just being left to rot.

My favorite feather is the one given to me by a man named Wolf, a Huron Indian and the son of Fred Wahpepah, an esteemed elder. He was the leader of the weekly Sweat Lodge I attended for a couple of years in Malibu on the family estate of Frank Lloyd Wright. When I moved to London, he gave me the feather for protection. It still hangs from my car's rearview mirror, and it always will.

I now live in a 750-acre bird preserve community called Audubon. A nesting pair of eagles live 200 feet from the house. They come every day to our lake to eat. Each season, they teach their young to fish and fly from the tree in our garden. The swamp adjoining our lake is an egret breeding ground; for two weeks in the spring, it is solid white and full of noise. Birds of all kinds fish at our lake every day.

As I sit on my lanai to watch, the birds keep a wary eye on me and hold tight to their wings! ✎

Feathering the Nest

Pam Owens

SEVERAL DECADES AGO, A YOUNG MEDICAL intern assigned to a large city hospital in Indianapolis went on an ambulance call to a poverty area. When he arrived, the intern was met at the door by two strapping young men with thick Ozark mountain accents. They explained that their sister was having a baby. When the intern examined her, he found that she was, indeed, in the late stages of labor and could not be moved. He gave instructions to the brothers to boil some water, and he began other preparations for a home delivery.

As the young doctor tended the mother-to-be, her brothers came in every two minutes or so to ask, "Is it time to feather her yet?"

The intern had no idea what that term meant, but he didn't want to anger the brothers, who clearly had a vested interest in making sure that the "feathering" would take place. Each time they asked, he would simply say, "No, not yet!"

Finally, though, he could put them off no longer and decided that whatever "feathering" was, it couldn't hurt at this point, since the baby was about to be born. The next time they asked, he told them, "Sure, go ahead—it's time now."

One of the brothers brought in a large feather and tickled his sister's nose with it. Sure enough, she sneezed, and, according to the good doctor, out popped the baby! ✎

Lynda's Magic Feather

Nancy Sena

MY SISTER LYNDA IS A FREE SPIRIT. SHE believes the universe will support her, and she wastes little energy on negatives.

She's driven a secondhand car for fifteen years, and she can't bear to part with it. Even in tropical Florida, she never uses its air conditioner. She likes nothing better than to feel the sun on her face and the wind in her hair, unless it's her daughter, Kelly, whom she loves unconditionally.

One evening we were loading some books and papers into Lynda's car. I noticed a yellow, emerald, and blue feather on the dusty console between the two front seats.

"What's with the feather?" I asked

"It's from Kelly's pet parrot," she said. "That bashful bird has taken a liking to me. This is my magic feather."

Several months later I had occasion to look in her car again. There lay the bright feather in the exact same spot.

"Did you glue that to the top of your console?" I asked.

"No," she smiled. "It stays right there with me. I told you, it's my magic feather!"

Sure enough, no matter how airy her old Toyota, no matter how many papers swirled out the open windows, the feather remained for months.

When one day it disappeared, Lynda merely shrugged and concluded that its magical powers had drifted on to someone who needed it more. ✎

Letting Go, Flying Free

Ron Yeomans

The blue feather in Illusions *didn't bother to explain itself to me. I watched while the story wrote itself through me and didn't get to ask questions.*

—Richard Bach

YEARS AGO, ONE OF MY FAVORITE BOOKS WAS *Illusions* by Richard Bach. The story is one of letting go of conditioned patterns and limitations, of trusting ourselves to make the right choices, and of learning unconditional love. At one point, Richard, the book's main character, decides to attract a blue feather by visualizing it, as "practice" for attracting whatever we want to happen in our lives.

The feather appeared on cue and demonstrated that we can choose to be powerfully connected to the universe—if we let go of what we *think* we know and let the forces of the universe lead us to truth.

Intellectually, I understood the message of *Illusions,* but it took me years to *feel* what Bach was saying and to apply it to my circumstances.

Twenty years later, blue feathers suddenly appeared everywhere in my life. A friend sent me a card—"out of the blue"—with a blue feather taped to it. A few mornings later, I found blue jay feathers lying on my deck as if they had been placed there deliberately. That same day, I received a postcard advertising a meeting on the topic "Synchronicity: Messages from the Universe." The postcard bore a blue jay stamp. I "got the message," attended the meeting, and began an exciting new spiritual journey.

Why, after all these years, I wondered, did blue feathers come into my life? What did they point to? Then I remembered Richard Bach's story. I took a close look at what my life had become.

What I saw was that I had been hanging on to old thoughts, judgments, habits. Something new needed to be born. These blue feathers urged me to let go, to fly away from what I had been clinging to that was no longer serving me, and to move on to receive and give unconditional, nonjudgmental love. Another book, *Conversations with God*, became the path to freedom that the blue feathers invited me to take.

Having spent my childhood in a repressive religious environment, I welcomed the *Conversations with God* book with open arms, an open mind, and an open heart. The concepts were clearly and compassionately stated. This was a God with whom I could identify, whom I could truly love, and who loved me unconditionally.

I'm learning to fly above all the things that

used to bother me so much. If I find myself holding back, being my old judgmental self, within a short time I come across a blue feather somewhere. It's as good as a stop sign. It's a message to hold up the mirror to myself instead of judging others.

Thank you, my blue-feathered friends, for reminding me of the oneness of our universe and for being fellow travelers on my path to understanding. My spirit flies with you. ❧

Meditation

A FISTFUL OF FEATHERS

Early this morning I walked down to the beach. I wasn't looking for feathers, just walking. But the feathers were there, wet and washed up along the shoreline, and I couldn't ignore them, could I? I kept picking them up, pelican feathers, gull feathers, even a heron feather or two.

Pretty soon I had a fistful of feathers—enough for a healing bundle, then enough to fill a large vase. I wasn't sure what to do with this gifting of feathers, nor did I know if they were truly meant as a message from the universe. They seemed like "ordinary" washed-up feathers. Still, I had never found this many before. The acquisitive side of me kept forcing feathers into my fist.

I walked farther and met a woman walking in the opposite direction who was picking up shells. She dragged a huge bag behind her, stuffing it with shells as she slowly shuffled forward, bending intently to the sand. I showed her my feathers; she showed me her shells. Then we parted, engrossed in adding to our respective collections.

One of yesterday's sandcastles had survived the night tides and sprawled before me. I had the urge to stick my feathers right on top of it. After all, a sandcastle is a sacred thing, too, something a child's mind (even in an adult's body!) builds out of nothing, knowing it won't last, knowing the sand ultimately belongs to the sea and not to the hands that shape it into towers and moats.

I thought of the birds that had shed these feathers. It was spring molting season. Perhaps they left these feathers behind so that newer, stronger ones could grow in. The birds seemed comfortable, too, with the idea of change and impermanence, with letting go of whatever was in the way of flying free and unencumbered.

One by one, I let my feathers drop from my hand. The morning tide would take care of them, as it would the sandcastles. They would soon return wholly to the earth and become soil again, as all things eventually do. Their sister feathers would ultimately join them, even the new ones just grown in.

Meanwhile, I felt lighter without the feathers I so fiercely clutched a few moments ago. I decided to take my feathers one at a time, and leave fistfuls to someone else.

What would lighten your load and help you fly free? Imagine yourself preparing for a long journey to the stars. What would you take with you that would help you fly faster and farther? What would you leave behind that would weigh you down?

Close your eyes, get quiet, let your fingers lie loose and open, and pose these questions

1. To your physical self
2. To your emotional self
3. To your mental self
4. To your spiritual self

Allow plenty of time for each of them to answer in their own ways. 🪶

Part Four

Where There's a Quill,

There's a Way!

Messages of Love, Strength,

and Courage

Remember Who You Are

Maril Crabtree

I'VE COME BACK TO THE BEACH. THE BEACH has always been a special place, a place of connection with Spirit, a place of peace. The endless murmur of Gulf waves calms me. It is a place to sit and listen, to let the buzzing doubts and fears recede with the retreating tide. It is a place to practice stillness, in the hope of arriving at the place of emptiness that is, paradoxically, the place of fullness.

Today, the sun hides behind scudding clouds and gray mist. Even the waves seem scruffy and lifeless, the shoreline bereft of the usual shell-seekers and strollers. Soon I grow restless. I need a sign that the universe is listening to me as deeply as I am listening to it. Still in a meditative space, I reach for my journal and wait for the pen to start moving. Soon it writes: "You will know when it is time to know. For now, continue on this path of sitting and listening. Be of good faith, be true to faith and say no to doubt. By that, we mean, simply, be true to yourself. Remember who you are. Your being is beautiful. Connect. Keep connecting."

I close the journal and walk slowly across the sand. I have asked for a sign, and the special sign for me is always a beautiful feather lying in my path.

But it is a windy day—so windy that most people have given up and left the beach. Those of us still here sit with our backs to the wind or walk briskly with heads lowered to avoid getting sand in our eyes. How can feathers land anywhere in this wind?

Finally, I see a bedraggled feather and pick it up. Thank you, Universe—I'll take it, even if it's not up to your usual pristine standards! Comforted, I walk on, intent on leaving the beach now that I have my sign.

I spot a ballpoint pen sticking out of the sand. Unusual. Maybe this, too, is a sign—to continue on the writing path. I bend to pick it up and glance at the clump of sea oats beside it. There, half-buried in the sand, is a large beautiful feather. Then I see a second perfect feather just inches from the first, gently waving in the wind, anchored by a few tufts of the sea oats.

"Okay, Okay, I get the message about saying no to doubt," I shout inwardly to the universe. I hear the gleeful reply: "Don't ever doubt that we can—and will—provide for you. Everything you desire is yours for the finding. Be open, and let the barrier of doubt disappear! Be assured that darkness and doubt return to light. Let the learning of love be your path. The love you seek is yours—is born within you. Love is who you are, and who you were meant to be. That is the true meaning of the feathers we send!"

Biblical Feathers

FROM GENESIS TO REVELATION, THE BIBLE is full of powerful and comforting images of birds, wings, and feathers. Here are a few selected passages.

* And God said, "Let the waters bring forth swarms of living creatures, and let birds fly above the earth across the firmament of the heavens. . . . And God blessed them, saying, "Be fruitful and multiply and fill the waters in the seas, and let birds multiply on the earth." *(Gen. 1:20, 22 Revised Standard Version)*

* He waited another seven days, and again he sent forth the dove out of the ark; and the dove came back to him in the evening, and lo, in her mouth a freshly plucked olive leaf; so Noah knew that the waters had subsided from the earth. *(Gen. 8:10–11 Revised Standard Version)*

* Like an eagle that stirs up its nest, that flutters over its young, spreading out its wings, catching them, bearing them on its pinions, the Lord alone did lead him. . . . *(Deut. 32:11–12 Revised Standard Version)*

* Is it by your wisdom that the hawk soars, and spreads his wings toward the south? Is it at your command that the eagle mounts up and makes his nest on high? *(Job 39:26–27 Revised Standard Version)*

- How precious is your constant love, O God! All humanity takes refuge in the shadow of your wings. *(Ps. 36:7 Living Bible Version)*
- And I said, Oh, that I had wings like a dove! for then would I fly away, and be at rest. *(Ps. 55:6 King James Version)*
- Let me dwell in thy tent forever! Oh to be safe under the shelter of thy wings! *(Ps. 61:4 King James Version)*
- Though ye have lien among the pots, yet shall ye be as the wings of a dove covered with silver, and her feathers with yellow gold. *(Ps. 68:13 King James Version)*
- Surely he shall deliver thee from the snare of the fowler, and from the noisome pestilence. He shall cover thee with his feathers, and under his wings shalt thou trust. . . . *(Ps. 91:3–4 King James Version)*
- If I take the wings of the morning and dwell in the uttermost parts of the sea, even there thy hand shall lead me, and thy right hand shall hold me. *(Ps. 139:9–10 Revised Standard Version)*
- Wilt thou set thine eyes upon that which is not? For riches certainly make themselves wings; they fly away as an eagle toward heaven. *(Prov. 23:5 King James Version)*
- But they that wait upon the Lord shall renew their strength; they shall mount up with wings as eagles; they shall run, and not be weary; and they shall walk, and not faint. *(Isa. 40:31 King James Version)*

- But for you who fear my name, the Sun of Righteousness will rise with healing in his wings. *(Mal. 4:2 Living Bible Version)*

- Look at the birds of the air: they neither sow nor reap nor gather into barns, and yet your heavenly Father feeds them.
  (Matt. 6:26 Revised Standard Version)

- And Jesus said to him, "Foxes have holes, and birds of the air have nests; but the Son of man has nowhere to lay his head."
  (Matt. 8:20 Revised Standard Version)

- And when he came up out of the water, immediately he saw the heavens opened and the Spirit descending upon him like a dove.
  (Mark 1:10 Revised Standard Version)

- Are not five sparrows sold for two farthings, and not one of them is forgotten before God?
  (Luke 12:6 King James Version)

- And the four living creatures, each of them with six wings, are full of eyes all round and within, and day and night they never cease to sing, "Holy, holy, holy, is the Lord God Almighty, who was and is and is to come!"
  (Rev. 4:8 Revised Standard Version)

Heirloom Feather

Carolyn Lewis King

FINDING A FEATHER IN YOUR FRONT YARD may not sound so miraculous, but the moment that I found my special feather stands out vividly in my memory.

First, you have to understand that my yard, like all the surrounding yards in the small Oklahoma town where I lived, was a barren expanse of brown grass. Nothing beautiful grew there. The pockets of natural gas underground, while not large enough to tap and produce income, made the soil inhospitable to most plants. The Oklahoma wind, irregular rainfall, and harsh climate kept our yard bleak and barren.

The next thing you need to know is that, through my mother's lineage, I am a member of the Bird Clan, part of the Muscogee Creek tribe. As a girl, I scanned the skies for an eagle or hawk, hoping a feather would bless me as it fell into my hands. I always knew that birds and their feathers were considered sacred and important in the ancient practices of my Clan.

My mother had been raised as a Christian. My father, also a full-blooded Muscogee Creek, refused to accept Christianity. He insisted on following the old ways—the spiritual ways of nature and religious ceremonies that had been passed on for generations by the tribe. I grew up attending Christian worship with my mother and also learning about nature and tribal ceremonies from my father's family. But, although I respected the old ways, I had never personally connected with them.

Now I was married and had a family of my own. We lived in a small house that stood in the middle of the original 160-acre allotment given to my husband's family over a hundred years ago, when our tribe was forced to move from its Alabama and Georgia homeland.

The door of our house faces east, the direction of the sunrise and, in Native American tradition, the direction of new beginnings, rebirth, and renewal. Each morning, as I left the house to head for the van I drove to pick up Head Start children, I spoke the prayers my father's family had taught me. Driving a van full of children was a big responsibility, and I always felt a little anxious. My prayers were simple: that it be a good day, and that we safely arrive at our destination. The hot August days trudged on, one following another, and I never knew whether my prayers made a difference.

One morning, I was more anxious than usual. I was running late, and as I faced east I prayed in a hasty, impatient way, then hopped into the van and backed it up to turn it toward the road.

That's when the feather appeared, a gleaming treasure in the middle of our barren yard. One minute the yard was the same as always, and the next minute it held this beautiful feather, about twelve inches long, a gift from the skies. Full of sudden joy, I leaped out of the van, picked it up, and cradled it in my hands. It was, for me, a sign to respect nature and to continue to respect the ancient ways as powerful and sacred.

For the first time, I received a direct sign of that power. The feather reassured me that my family—my children and my children's children—would have access to the Spirit by strengthening our connections with nature.

The feather is still with me. I keep it on a special shelf. It has been used to bless my house and the homes and lives of others. My children have used it in school plays (my grandson, who is seven, is the latest family member to use it in a school play). The feather occupies a place of honor in their hearts as it does in mine. It's as much of a family heirloom as a piece of jewelry or furniture, reminding me that our family stretches across time and in all four directions, as far as the eye can see and as wide as the heart can hold.

Feather Magic

Robert M. "Bob" Anderson, Ph.D.

I FOUND MYSELF IN THE WORLD OF THE LATE eighties with a complete loss of identity and direction. My first marriage had ended. I was living in a small town in rural Louisiana, trying to gather my energies to begin again. My professional life was in upheaval; my personal life was a disaster. Nothing looked promising on the horizon, and I was in serious depression. That's when my first significant experience with feathers happened.

Part of my daily routine, despite my depression, was a three-mile jog. I ran a three-mile circle on a country road, starting at my house. Before I ran, I always drew a line in the dirt in front of my house, as my start and finish line. The road was usually deserted, except for an occasional car. Along the way, tall pines, hickory trees, and oaks lined the road. A section of wetlands edged up to one section of the road, and I sometimes saw egrets, herons, and other water birds.

On this particular day, I was running because I could not think of anything else to do. The constant rhythmic pounding, though, was not driving away my demons. I still felt depressed and lost. Tears ran down my face as I jogged. I barely noticed the beauty of the deserted road. Occasionally I heard the mournful cries of mockingbirds; they seemed to mock my tears and loneliness. About halfway through my run, I remember thinking, "I could really use some magic in my life."

Richard Bach's book, *Illusions*, floated through my mind. I had read it two years before and was deeply moved by it. I decided to see if I could "magnetize" a blue feather. Following the instructions outlined in the book, I closed my eyes, pictured the feather in my hand, and surrounded it in golden light. Then I emptied everything out of my mind and ran and ran and ran.

By the time I finished the run, I felt like I was flying, I was running so hard. When I crossed the "start/finish" line I'd drawn in the dirt, I almost stumbled in shock. There was a feather lying right on the line!

I ran past the line a few feet and slowly walked back. I stood there for several minutes, just looking at the feather. When I picked it up, my shock doubled—I had never seen a feather like this. It was a brilliant deep blue. The reverse side was a beautiful gold.

Several months later, I was teaching karate near a pet store. During a break, I went inside and saw a macaw. That's when I knew that the feather I had magnetized that day belonged to a macaw—a bird I had never before seen.

I know many things can be explained, but I'll leave it to you to decide what the odds are that a macaw would drop a blue feather on a line I drew in the sand on a dirt road in rural Louisiana on the very day I decided to magnetize one.

Today we live in a world in which there are few heroes, no magic, no wonder, and, for many, no future. That day, the magic of the universe happened to me. Not to someone else. To me. I cannot deny it, and I'll never forget it. The message that day was simple: Magic exists. You can't explain it, you can't control it. If you could, it would not be magic; it would be science.

The blue feather is a tangible reminder of what I can't see and can't imagine or understand. I am an old cop and I believe in evidence. The blue feather for me is magic, good luck, positive forces, and evidence. It allows me sometimes to go to a place I need to be and be reminded of what I most need to remember.

Ritual

FEATHER-BREATH

With thanks to my friend Saphira who first suggested this ritual.

* Decide what intention you want to place into the universe.
* Take a feather (the larger, the better) and clean the end that would normally be attached to a bird (the part used to make quill pens).
* Hold the feather in your hands with the hollow-tube quill end close to your lips. Fill this hollow tube with your intention by breathing into it several times while focusing on the words of your intention. *Example:* "I am filled with courage/love/understanding as this feather is filling with my breath."

    You can also do the reverse by filling the hollow tube end with your intention to release something you no longer want or need in your life. *Example:* "I am releasing my anger/hatred/fear as I fill this feather with my breath."

* Close your eyes and concentrate on what you are sending forth as you hold the feather lightly in your palm. Fill it with your energy, along with your intention.
* When you sense that the message has been received, give thanks for the feather as your willing instrument.
* If you wish, place the feather in a prominent place where it will be visible to you often as a reminder of your intention. Or you can simply place the feather in one of your favorite nature-spots and let it do its work from there.

A Gift of Love

Aweisle Epstein

A field of feathers for the strife of love.
—Luis De Gongora Y Argote,
Soledad, I

I WAS AT A THREE-MONTH-LONG MEDITATION retreat, with a hundred or so other people, in the foothills of California's Sierras. My fiancé of six months was there, too, but in another program. After he had been away six weeks for initial training, I joined him for the rest of the course, eager to be near him again.

Though his scheduled activities differed from mine, it would have been possible for us to sit together at meals but such was not to be. Unaccountably, he seemed to be avoiding me and appeared to be quite entranced by another woman who was taller and thinner than I. Her smile seemed brighter and her blue eyes twinkled whenever she spoke to him. It seemed to me that they always sat together at mealtimes, and I often saw them walking off toward the forest together during breaks.

If by chance (or design), I encountered him alone on the pathway on his way to or from the commons area, he seemed aloof—or not interested in talking to me—in sharp contrast to the soft radiance that illumined his face whenever he joined her.

This was a trial I was not prepared for. All my life

I had waited for this man. From the first moment of our meeting, our souls had seemed to jump toward each other and mingle in a little cloud over our heads. We were on the same spiritual path. We had declared our love for each other and made plans to get married, have children, and spend our lives together.

Within a few days, I found myself sobbing uncontrollably in the privacy of my room. My heart seemed likely to break I wanted so badly to talk to him, but he was never available. The more I tried to reach to him, the more unreachable he became.

I tried to think of excuses to talk to him, and left a note outside his door. "May I borrow your *I Ching?*" He had someone else bring it to me. I left him another note. "Can we get together for a half hour before dinner? I want to return your book, and I need to talk to you." His answering note: "I'm too busy with the course. Leave the book with Bob (one of his two teachers)."

Then one cold, snowy December day, as I sat in meditation, someone slid an envelope under the door. The message was in his elegant handwriting. "I was walking through the woods, asking God for a sign of His love . . . and these floated down to my feet. I thought you would appreciate the symbolism."

Tucked in the envelope were two soft fluffy cream-colored feathers, each with a darker heart centered on the feather, like the under feathers of barn owls. (Neither of us knew it at the time, but owls of all kinds are devoted lifelong mates.)

A year later we were married, and twenty-three years later we are still utterly devoted to each other. ✍

Feathers and Stones
Maril Crabtree

Like a stone it sinks
To the bottom of my soul.
"Unworthy" dwells there.
Like a stone it sits
In the middle of my heart.
"Unworthy" rests there.

Comes the feather now
Floating down onto the stone.
"Most holy" calls there.
Comes the feather now
To cradle ancient stone.
"Most holy" speaks there.

Carve stone with feather:
Beauty of wholeness.
Carve stone with feather:
Birth love with boldness.

Carve stone with feather:
True self unfolded.

Crow Medicine

Gaylen Ariel

It is not only fine feathers that make fine birds.
—Aesop

IN THE MID-1990S I SPENT SOME TIME IN THE
mountains, in the process of healing myself from a
life-altering trauma. Mother Earth has never failed
to be there when I open my heart to her, and this
crucial time proved no exception.

I was reading about crow medicine and noticed
that each day a circle of crows would fly over the area
I was visiting. Gradually, I understood that I would
be protected by the crow as long as I needed it.

Just before leaving the area to return home, I
saw a crow feather standing straight up in the pebble
driveway of my friends' home where I was staying.
"What a nice gift . . . What a nice coincidence," I
thought. When I told my friends about it, they were
even more skeptical that it really meant anything.

But when we drove to the airport a couple of
days later for my return flight, we changed our
minds. One of my friends drove and parked in the
covered garage parking lot. While I sat in the car,
he walked around to the passenger side. Instead of
opening my door, he motioned for me to roll down
the car window. When I did, he leaned over and

presented me with a crow feather that he had found lying right next to my car door.

"Another coincidence?" he smiled quizzically.

"I don't even want to talk about it," I said.

Back home, things seemed easier and I continued to keep my crow feathers around for a sense of calm and protection. A few weeks later, I walked to my solid metal mailbox to retrieve my mail. I opened the mailbox door and out flew an entire crow. Yes, a very alive, very alert crow!

I have seen a great many things beyond my comprehension, but even by my standards having a live crow fly out of my mailbox is, as they say, one for the books. I stood there for a few moments, trying to catch my breath. When I finally reached in to get my mail, I realized I had been given yet another gift of a feather.

I must add yet another crow incident to a story I thought was finished. When I got ready to print out this story for the first time, I found that my ink cartridge was empty. I walked outside to get into my car to go purchase another one.

I heard them before I saw them. A cacophony of calls led me to look up and see at least sixty crows circling over my head. Not surprising? It is if you don't live in crow country!

I will always treasure my crow feathers and give thanks for the protection I felt during that difficult time of my life. To this day, wherever I am I look down at my feet and should there be a feather, I say, "Thank you for your gift!"

Swan Story

Antoinette Botsford

MY GRANDFATHER WAS ATHABASKAN/BEAVER Clan on his mother's side and French-Canadian/ Metis on his father's side. He was raised Catholic and knew little of his ancestral spiritual traditions. Like so many youngsters of native heritage, he was seduced by spirits in the bottle at an early age and succumbed to alcohol-related causes before I could know him. But as I grew up, I became more and more curious about the Metis part of our heritage.

I learned that traditionally my grandfather's people had special coming-of-age observations that involved initiation into something that would perhaps translate as "the Order of the Swan."

Swan medicine, according to tribal lore, was particularly helpful to young men and women making the transition from childhood to adulthood. The attributes of the swan contributed to their transition as responsible tribal members: swans are loyal to their mates lifelong, fly in groups, return always to certain lakes at certain times of the year, trumpet when necessary but are mostly silent, and swim for long hours in cold water (a purification ritual among many native people).

Every young person, I was told, who had successfully gone through the "ordeals" involved in becoming a young man or young woman would have some swan feathers tied over their sleeping place or in their medicine bundle. Maybe having a swan feather and being a "swan-child" helped people keep their agreements to be temperate and moderate and enduring in their life.

Pondering this new information, I went walking, one bleak December afternoon, with my husband along the shore of a lake not far from where we live. Eight trumpeter swans had recently arrived from Canada to make the lake their winter refuge.

"How wonderful it would be to have a swan feather, in honor of my grandfather's people," I thought. And there, in the cold water some twenty feet or so into the lake, came floating a swan feather!

But it moved no nearer to the shore, and the day was too cold to consider a swim, especially at our age.

"Would you like that feather?" asked my husband.

"Oh yes," I said.

"I will get it for you."

"No, don't. You'll make yourself ill with cold."

"Watch me," he said.

He picked up a stone and threw it so that it landed in the water some distance—perhaps twenty-five feet—away from us. The stone entered the still gray lake with a *plop*, and, of course, created concentric rings of water. The stone's impact made the water move enough that the feather was pushed along, gently, on the surface, closer to the shore. He did this one more time, and the feather came in so close that with a big reach he claimed it and gave it to me.

Need I say that this is among the most precious of my rather large feather collection? 🖋

Feather Angel

Kara Ciel Black

MY FRIEND MELISSA AND I DECIDED TO GO on a grand adventure—a bicycle trip from my home in Seattle to San Francisco. We had no mishaps while we traveled through Washington State. Both roads and drivers were biker-friendly. We rode all day, passing through the towering forests of the Cascades, and camped at night.

But things changed when we got to California. At times, drivers intentionally tried to crowd us off the road. The shoulders were narrower, grades sharper, and drop-offs steeper. Our adventurous ride became an anxious journey as we sought to protect ourselves from vehicles that seemed determined to run us down.

As we crested a long hill, our trip suddenly became a nightmare. We pedaled across a long bridge over a river canyon. I was riding in front, with Melissa about half a mile back, still toiling up the hill. As I glanced down to my right, nothing separated me from a big drop-off except a narrow shoulder and a two-foot guardrail. Just then a big eighteen-wheeler crested the hill, passed us, and immediately pulled over to the shoulder and braked right in front of us. Oncoming traffic streamed by and there was no way to get around the truck. Its huge rear end loomed closer every second.

Panicked, I braked as hard as I could. I knew I had only three choices: (1) veer off to the right and be flipped over the guardrail to the canyon below, which would almost certainly mean death; (2) plow into the back of the truck, which would result in serious injury at best; or (3) get my bike stopped before I hit the truck and became human roadkill.

At the last possible second, my bike came to a stop, inches from the back of the truck. I barely heard it start up. The roaring in my head mingled with the sound of gears grinding as the truck went on its way. The driver had had his fun and didn't stick around for the aftermath.

I was still shaking, straddling my bike, when Melissa caught up to me. She had witnessed the whole thing and was shaking, too—with anger as well as fear. She dismounted and came over to me, hugging me as the tears of relief and anger finally started down my face.

Just then, the stranger whom I refer to only as my "road angel" pulled up to us. He climbed out and hurried over. He, too, had seen the whole thing.

"Are you all right?" he asked, his face full of concern. His deep brown eyes were warm and friendly, with faint "laugh lines" fanning out, and his dark hair was pulled back into a long ponytail. His bronze skin had the rugged look of a man who spends time outdoors, doing his own chores.

We assured him that we were physically okay, but he could see that we were still shaken emotionally. We continued talking.

"I live down by the river, just at the bottom of this canyon," he said. "Would you like to take a break before you continue your trip, and just relax, have a cup of tea?"

Without hesitation, we both agreed. Somehow we knew that we could trust this kind stranger. He picked up our bikes and put them in the back of his battered pickup camper. We joined him in the cab and drove the short distance down a winding road to his house, which was, as he had said, right on the river.

It was a small house, but a deep sense of peace filled the room we sat in. He insisted that we sit and rest while he prepared tea. Then we went out to the porch and looked at the river and the deep woods surrounding us as we talked. Gradually, my fear and anger subsided, and my normal buoyant self returned.

A couple of hours later, we stood to leave.

"Before you go, I want you to have these." He disappeared into the house, then came back out with something in each hand.

"These are medicine bundles. I made them myself. They'll protect you for the rest of your trip."

The medicine bundle he handed me was three leather pouches, woven together with rope. Hanging from the bundle were several large feathers in beautiful colors, each from a different bird. He told us that the feathers had come from roadkill, and that he had given the birds a proper burial, purifying and blessing them and honoring their spirits. He pointed out the various types of feathers and told us something about the spiritual energy of each.

The feathers swayed in the breeze, and their movement seemed a reassurance that the spirits of the birds that had contributed them would be watching over us to make sure that we didn't become roadkill, too. We made the rest of the trip in perfect safety.

At home, the medicine bundle hangs from my door, where the feathers move and sway each time it opens and closes, a gentle reminder of the hospitality of a stranger and a continued blessing and source of protection in my life. ✐

Inner Space

Mary-Lane Kamberg

Struggling to be average I
spin like a feather
in an eclectic orbit
of trips to the bank and grocery
and endless loads of laundry
my life is making sausage
stuffing forgettable bits and pieces
into a crowded place
I turn my face to the wall
and in my head write poems
that will last as long as memory

One Feather
at a Time

Kimball C. Brooks

'Hope' is the thing with feathers —
That perches in the soul —
  —Emily Dickinson

IT WAS SPRING AND I WAS A PATIENT IN AN alcoholic rehabilitation center. I had been there one week and I was terrified, lonely, and confused. I could not bear the thought that I could never drink again. I was told that I had to change everything about the way I perceived my life. Over and over again, I heard that I had to change my attitude and find a God of my understanding.

There was a large pond on the grounds of the center. It was a home for several geese families. Each day during our free time, I went there to walk and try to make sense of what was happening to me. I was drawn to this pond, although I didn't know why. My heart was so heavy and full of fear that I could never make all of these changes.

One day, as I walked around the pond with my head down, I saw a feather on the ground before me. The tip of the feather was black. The feather gradually turned to gray and then to white, with soft down tufts at the quill end.

Suddenly a new thought came to me: Maybe I didn't have to change abruptly. Like the feather, I, too, could grow from the darkness into the light gradually. For the first time, I understood the concept I'd heard repeatedly, that is the cornerstone of recovering alcoholics everywhere—one day at a time. For the first time, I had a feeling of hope that I could actually change and accept a life without drinking.

I still have that feather as a reminder. I have put those "one day at a time" days into fifteen years, and my soul is as soft and peaceful as that white down on my feather. ✍

Meditation

An Unexpected Gift

My friend Deborah and I walk together as often as we can. Today we experienced one of those walks that goes nowhere and everywhere, a walk where every footstep traverses new ground over trails you think will be familiar.

As we walked, we also talked. We let our lives reveal themselves to each other in new and unexpected ways. The walk became a journey into unknown territory, finding unanticipated answers to previously pondered questions, finding more questions, seeing things from different perspectives.

At the end of our time together, we turned off the sidewalk onto the walkway to her home. She went ahead a few steps to unlock the door. As I slowly followed her, I looked down and saw a small brown feather gleaming at me from the middle of the walk, lying underside up.

The underside of a feather looks the same, yet different. Its sheen is greater, the color lighter and more uniform, the shape slightly concave, with edges curling up instead of down.

As I turned the feather over and over in my hand, I saw dozens of subtle differences in the two sides. I had never stopped to examine the underside of a feather, just as I don't usually take the time to look at my life from that perspective. The same yet different: the surprising gift of the unexpected that was there all along.

Yet when the universe unexpectedly hands me something sorrowful or unpleasant, I don't usually treat it as a welcome gift. I react to whatever is happening as if it had only one side, the presenting side, the side that leaves me with clipped wings and a heavy heart.

It takes time—sometimes a long time—to remember to look at the underside, to seek the hidden meanings, to find the secret gifts of what came into my life. Instead, I hide my head under my wing and hop along looking only at the ground, forgetting for the moment that I can still fly, can still lift myself to another place and another perspective. From ground height, a pebble looks like a boulder; from the air, that same pebble is barely noticeable.

I'm learning to see the power in the unknown, the hidden, the places of life that don't always follow the rational, logical path but, instead, wander through many twists and turns. Everything has an underside. Birds couldn't fly without both sides of their wings; neither can we. I'm learning to appreciate the beauty of *both* sides.

* Choose a familiar object that you use or pass by every day, either in your home or in your yard—one small enough to hold in your hand. Find a comfortable place to sit with the object.

* Close your eyes for a moment and envision yourself with the ability to have x-ray vision, seeing into and through the object, seeing it in different colors and from different angles, and so on.

* Open your eyes and look at the object from this new perspective. Note all the things you never noticed before: texture, smell, how the shape feels. Let the object guide you in other things to notice about it.

* Think of a time in your past when something sad or unpleasant happened. From the perspective of the present, what unexpected, hidden gifts have emerged?

* Now close your eyes and put yourself forward in time another decade. From the perspective of that "future," what other gifts do you see?

Eagle Medicine

Maya Trace Borhani

The day is done, and the darkness
Falls from the wings of Night,
As a feather is wafted downward
From an eagle in his flight.
—Henry W. Longfellow, *"The Day Is Done"*

FEATHERS OFTEN MARK THE PATH WHEN transformation is afoot, flying in from windows opening out into other realms. Harbingers of memory and intuition, symbols of transformation and rebirth, these gifts arrive as spirit manifest, reminding me of sacred medicine ways.

Living on an island off the coast of Washington State, a wilderness of sea surrounds me and the deluxe bird menagerie that also homes here. Heron and kingfisher, osprey and cormorant populate island beaches, skies, and waterways. Clambering up rocky, rose-and-lichen-strewn cliffs, I've lain for hours on a mossy bed over-looking an eagle's nest, contemplating the flight of watchful parents to and fro. The glittering, green-apple sea lies far below, teeming with life, sustenance for this place.

One summer's full moon night, I climbed the 1,500-foot crest of the seaward-facing Entrance

Mountain, a vigorous hike up sheer flanks to reach a circle of stones at the top. With views of the Cascades to the east, the Olympic range to the south, and Canada's silhouette to the west, I was on top of my visible world and sovereign to its majesty. I had made the climb, a familiar day hike, this time to say farewell; life was leading me away from my island home and the sanctuary it had become.

At the last steep incline before reaching the top, I looked off to the west under the sweeping canopy of an ancient maple tree, into the mostly starlit evening air. A bright feather caught my eye there, sticking straight up out of the ground. Scrambling along the traverse, rocks sliding away at my feet, I came to the small, still downy feather and freed it from its corporeal embrace.

Richly mottled white with dark brown, it held a wide arc and was light and soft. This was my first eagle's feather, a symbol of power in a time of transition and change; a signal to go ahead, trust the journey, take the next step. All night long, beneath August's incandescent full moon glow, that feather crowned the mountaintop altar where I slept, spiriting me onward.

Now, after much journeying, I am back in my island home. Change and transformation have been my steady companions, and I have returned here instinctively, not understanding fully what mysterious pulls are guiding my life. Past and present intersect, and sometimes collide, with me walking between them into my future, into the unknown. The land, the elements, the breath of life carries me through.

Out walking this winter through a brightly lit, windy forest, I headed to gale-buffeted grassy bluffs above the water. The wind was fierce at the water's edge, equal to the sun's unseasonable warmth on my face. I had come this tempestuous day to bury what remained of trinkets once showered on me by a former love. I wanted to sit and muse, to contemplate the turbulent waves, such a rarity in this region of flat serene waters. I kept walking along moss-laden cliffs, looking for a niche in the rock that would allow me to soak up the precious sunlight while shielding me from the wind's pursuit. Finally I found a crevasse I could nestle into and imbibe the sun's warmth.

The rhythm of non-thought held sway. I relished lying there on the earth, my own wiry body conforming to her bony frame, rocks like arms holding me, this welcoming back always the best lover. Tears welled, as I expected. I wanted to release the attachment that bound me to symbols of love, to release what caged my own capacity to love now.

These were not tears of sadness, so much as a terrific kind of purge, blessing, acknowledgment, and renewal. Memories of one man's ways, of a love that I expect will never exactly go away, of things that had come between us, and things that will probably forever bind us, danced in my mind.

I had finally survived the healing of time, mistrusted but accurate truism that it is. I felt a delicious awareness born of experience, the impenetrable mystery of paradox, and this gift of life upon the earth. I knew that joy was supreme, that even loss and sorrow must be put down in order to walk fully in the beauty to which we are born.

It was time to go. I had done what I came to do. I stood up and turned on my heel to walk rapidly up behind where I had lain. The trail back led down along the rock face, the other way; but some mysterious force compelled me to climb over the patches of delicate moss, away from the water and toward the forest's edge.

At the top of the rock, where it dropped off into scrub and thorn below, I saw at my feet a feather embedded slightly in the deep moss. I reached down and gently loosed the young eagle feather from its nesting place. I recognized the stately breadth, large quill, and faint mottling of white at the feather's base. Eagle medicine, initially clearing me for takeoff, was now a symbol of sovereignty in myself, companion to my strong heart quest. I knelt on the wet moss and wept and laughed for this affirmation that in letting go I will not fall, but fly—or at least float!

A voice inside, that I heard all around me in the branches and breeze and rocks where I stood, said, "With understanding comes wisdom, and treasures of the earth to mark our sight. Be aware," it continued. "Note what is around you. See all that you are, and feel, and become, in every piece of nature that surrounds you. Be as one."

If Birds Can Fly

Marty Peach

FOR YEARS, TO CAMOUFLAGE MY TREMENDOUS fear of flying, I would have several drinks of alcohol before and during these flights. I needed to be brain-dead to fly. Before I admitted my alcoholism and got help, I had killed quite a few brain cells both on the ground and in the air.

I was sober for about five years before I could get up the courage to try flying without alcohol. Now that drinking could no longer be part of my life, I had to fly sober and fly alone!

The big test came when I was getting ready for my trip to India. To tour this vast mysterious land had always been my dream, but I wasn't sure I could handle the many hours of flying. To add to my stress, I was concerned about leaving my three cockatoos to a bird sitter. My "feathered family" had become an important part of my life and my recovery. These three beautiful birds gave me many hours of joy, and I had bonded as closely with them as many people do with their pet cats or dogs.

I was in tears while driving myself to the airport, parking the car, and rushing to the ticket counter. Doubt and fear had already set in. I felt so anxious and alone. How would I manage this monumental flight without the aid of alcohol? I was determined to go, but the thought of going through with it had me quaking inside.

Finally it was my turn at the ticket counter. When I reached inside my purse for my ticket, out of the recesses flew this lovely peach-colored feather. I knew immediately it was from my Moluccan cockatoo, Peaches. I had no idea, however, how it ended up in my purse.

As the feather fluttered slowly down onto the counter, a wonderful sense of peace and calm came over me. With a sense of joy now replacing the fear, the thought came to me: "I can do this!" I knew my birds would be fine, and I would be, too.

That peaceful feeling stayed with me throughout my time in India. It was reinforced when, partway through the trip, a tour companion said, "Marty, look down." There at my feet was the most extraordinary peacock feather.

I still have these two beautiful feathers. They are a powerful reminder of the day-by-day surrender at the heart of my recovery, and a reminder that I am never alone. For this, I am most grateful.

Chief Mini-feather

Phillip G. Crabtree

ONE EVENING AFTER RETURNING HOME FROM
music rehearsal, I went to my room as I always do
to clean my guitar. I took my guitar out of its case
and got out my old T-shirt to polish it before putting it away. My grandfather gave me this shirt on
a vacation in the Caribbean Islands when I was
only nine. It had a cartoon caricature of a yellow
duck wearing oversized sunglasses on it. In one
lens of the glasses there was an image of the island
of Martinique and in the other lens was a picture of
St. Martin.

Long after I outgrew the shirt, I kept it
around because of its sentimental value. When
music and guitars became a special part of my life,
its softness from being washed so many times made
it ideal for a polishing cloth.

My grandfather, Corbin Meriwether, had died
several years before. We had always been close.
The vacation we took together was typical of the
good times we had, especially after I turned seven.
That was the year my parents divorced and also
the year my grandmother died. We both had big,
empty voids in our lives and grew closer than we
had ever been before. From then on, we were the
best of friends.

When we were together, it seemed to make the

troubles of the world seem small. Often, we would go to wildlife retreats, hiking, or bird watching, or I would just sit back and listen to his wonderful stories about life. He was a kind man, full of good humor and a lighthearted approach to life, always ready with a smile for me.

I had been polishing my guitars for years with this T-shirt, so it was unusual for me to think of my grandfather when I used it. On this particular night, when I saw the shirt, I stopped and reflected on the memories of the good times he and I had spent together.

Lately, I had been having some tough times. I was approaching my thirtieth birthday. Throughout that year, I had been feeling a little down. It was the first year of my life that I realized a few signs of aging were evident; when I looked in the mirror, I saw a few streaks of gray here and there. Several of my dear friends and relatives had died, and I felt more alone. I reflected on my life and felt that I had fallen short of where I wanted to be.

All these thoughts ran through my mind as I polished with the faded T-shirt of my youth. After I put away my guitar, I turned around and immediately noticed a tiny white feather, fluffy and brilliant, no bigger than a thumbnail, lying in the middle of my bedroom floor. When I walked over to it, I was overwhelmed with a feeling of the presence of my grandfather. It felt as though he were present in the room, speaking directly to me.

I knew he could tell that I had been hurting

inside for quite a while. In that moment, I heard his voice echoing inside me, telling me that he was with me, and always had been, and that life is about living now, not in the past or future.

"One day we'll be together again," his final words echoed inside me.

In that brief moment, everything changed. I'm not sure what was stirred inside me, but I felt like I could see things in a different perspective. The feeling of aloneness was gone, and I no longer felt down and depressed. A sense of warmth and comfort filled me.

Later that night, I searched my entire room to see if the feather could have come from something I had, but I found nothing. When I mentioned the strange phenomenon to my mother over the phone the next evening, she told me something I never knew.

"You know, your grandfather was quite a punster," she said. "One of his jokes when I was a little girl was to call himself 'Chief Mini-feather.' It was his favorite nickname."

I have since retired the T-shirt; it had served its purpose well. Although the presence of my grandfather that night was brief, its uplifting impact on me will last for a lifetime. I don't so much see things with my eyes anymore; rather, I see and feel more with my heart. All these feelings were triggered by a loving grandfather and the tiniest white angel of a feather. That tiny white feather became my talisman to remind me that life is good, and I'm not alone.

What Ties Me to the Earth Is Unseen

Mark Nepo

My heart was beating like a heron awakened
in the weeds, no room to move. Tangled
and surprised by the noise of my mind,
I fluttered without grace to the center
of the lake which humans call silence.

I guess if you should ask, peace
is no more than the underside
of tired wings resting on the lake
while the heart in its feathers
pounds softer and softer.

The Courage of the Eagle

Gerald Wagner

OF ALL FEATHERS, THE EAGLE FEATHER IS THE most highly prized in both Native American tradition and in contemporary tribal custom. It is revered as a sacred symbol of the great bird itself and of its strength, power, and endurance.

In many Native American tribes, an ancient warrior's tradition known as "counting coup" existed. To get close enough to touch an armed enemy with a special stick called a coup stick or with the hand and escape was considered an even greater feat than killing him. Counting coup was an act of daring that often called for more courage than killing someone from a safe hiding spot.

A warrior who successfully counted coup was honored and acknowledged by his tribal peers with eagle feathers, a sign of their great courage. The eagle feathers were tied into the hair and worn with great pride. Chiefs and other recognized leaders accumulated enough feathers to create an entire headdress, worn for ceremonial occasions and in battle.

The old tradition of "counting coup" has a modern twist throughout many tribal reservations today—at college graduation ceremonies where

Native American graduates are honored. Graduates are given an eagle feather as a symbol of honor and courage to acknowledge achievement in completing all the requirements for a college degree. It has become the custom to tie this feather onto the tassel of the mortarboard and to wear it during the graduation ceremony itself.

I received my eagle feather from a friend who is a traditional dancer, using feathers in the dances that have been performed for hundreds of years. Knowing that it has been part of those dances made it even more of an honor to receive. After graduation, I had the end of my feather beaded and it now hangs on my wall as a reminder of what I've achieved.

The tradition of wearing eagle feathers and other Native American traditional dress at graduation becomes more elaborate with advanced degrees. People with master's degrees may bead their whole cap, and people with a doctorate often wear full traditional Native American dress.

Ethel Connally Johnson, the first Native American woman to receive a doctorate from Colorado State University School of Veterinary Medicine, wanted to honor her Native American ancestry at her graduation. Several weeks before graduation ceremonies, Ethel made a formal request to the dean of the College of Veterinary Medicine for permission to wear her tribe's traditional clothing during the ceremony. The dean denied her request.

At the graduation ceremony, Ethel filed in, in cap and gown, and waited for her name to be called. She then stood up, unzipped her gown, and stepped out of it. Beneath the gown she wore a deerskin dress adorned with feathers, beads, and the jewelry that had been in her family for generations. As she walked to the podium to receive her degree, she also received a standing ovation from the entire audience.

Whenever I think of her, I think of a woman who had the courage to honor herself and her people—not for the purpose of going against the power of the "establishment," but simply to honor her ancestors. She had the courage of the eagle.

In Memoriam

K. M. Jordan

FOR MANY YEARS, I HAVE COLLECTED feathers. Some I purchased, but most were gifts from above. Feathers have always had a special place in my life. As a child, I always wanted to fly. I guess I'm an eagle at heart—I've always been a person of strong spirit and a leader who leads by example. I love to "fly" by reaching for something new.

My younger brother also had the heart of an eagle. He had a great love for the outdoors and moved to Montana in the mid-1970s, getting a job with the Forestry Service so he could be outdoors every day. He spent most of the time working on the trails in an area known as the Scapegoat Wilderness, just north of Helena. He loved the mountains, the wilderness, and the solitude. Like the eagle, he possessed extraordinary strength and courage.

A few years ago, my brother died of complications from scleroderma. He spent the last month of his life confined to a hospital bed. When his spirit was finally released from its physical confinement, I decided to travel to the mountains and spread his ashes where he had lived and worked for so many years. But I knew that leaving his ashes would not be enough. I decided to create a feather bundle in his memory, to leave in the place where I planned to spread his ashes.

I read books on sacred ceremonies and Native American traditions. I couldn't find instructions anywhere, so I asked for guidance to create the feather bundle and the ceremony, and to make the preparations for the trip. The process took several months and allowed time for my own healing.

As I gathered items to honor him, several people donated gifts when they heard what I was doing, and I felt Spirit working through them to provide what was needed. I would have liked to have had an eagle feather for the bundle, but since I am not Native American, I chose the noble turkey instead. I symbolically tied the turkey feathers into my brother's hair, pointing down, which indicated that he was a man of honor.

For the ceremony itself, I chose a place Karl had often talked about, near a small cabin on Webb Lake. I burned sage and smudged the four directions as well as above and below, then purified myself. I sprinkled the ground with sea salt and yellow and blue cornmeal in a circle.

After I had dug a small hole in the circle, I leaned up against a large pine tree and listened to the wind singing in the trees, feeling complete peace. Karl had sent many pictures of this area, which was home to a Forestry Service line camp. The sky was deep blue with large white clouds billowing all around. I could see why Karl loved that spot so much. I closed my eyes and pictured him, free of disease and suffering, flying with his beloved eagles at last.

Then I placed the things I had gathered, one by one, into the bundle: the turkey feathers; a red stone horse fetish; stones of crystal, turquoise, rose quartz, and amethyst quartz; macaw feathers; and tobacco and cornmeal. I presented each item in prayer, asking the Great Spirit to bless Karl and to release his spirit to do his next great work.

A new sense of peace came over me as I completed the ceremony. I continue to be blessed with feathers. Each time they appear, I think of Karl and feel close to him. Someday we'll fly together again.

Sophia's Gift

Sheelagh G. Manheim, Ph.D.

My brother used to ask the birds to forgive him; that sounds senseless but it is right; for all is like the ocean, all things flow and touch each other; a disturbance in one place is felt at the other end of the world.
— Dostoyevsky, *The Brothers Karamazov*

FEATHERS HAVE ALWAYS BEEN BIG IN MY LIFE. As a child I collected them because of their beauty. I would move them through the air, stroke my cheek with them, press the little bits together to make them one, gather them together to make a fan. To find a feather was to find a treasure, to feel special.

In my adult years, after I experienced Jungian analysis and became a Jungian psychotherapist, I learned to see the world symbolically, and my love of feathers took on a whole new meaning. Feathers were still a gift from heaven, but now they also became messages to my soul.

This became most real to me during one summer I spent on Martha's Vineyard. We had had ten days of constant rain and I was very depressed. The afternoon the sun finally came out, I left the house and walked to the duck pond. In fact, I was more than depressed. The thought of just walking into the tranquil pond and never emerging drew me to pace up and down the bank of the pond, singing a hymn to Sophia, goddess of wisdom.

Gazing at the pond as I paced, I saw what seemed to be a miniature catamaran swooping across the water toward me, blown by the wind. I was captivated to discover that it was not a child's toy, but rather two large swan feathers, parallel in the water, with their quill ends up. They were driving across the pond directly toward me. I waited quietly, my heart full of joy, all thoughts of ending my life gone. The feathers bumped against the bank, and I gratefully reached to claim Sophia's gift to me.

Every summer after that, it seemed my prayers were answered by the gift of feathers from a bird that represented the answer to my soul's question. One year I was exploring the idea of dignity. I found wild turkey feathers of many kinds and was finally granted the ultimate gift of the presence of the wild turkeys. Another summer, I was recovering from Lyme disease and I found beautiful feathers of the guinea fowl. They eat the ticks responsible for spreading the Lyme spirochete. I then received the gift of seeing a flock of guinea fowl eating their way across our meadow.

Crow feathers, owl feathers, redbird feathers—all have been, at various times, gifts to my soul to help me understand life and learn the lessons I needed to learn. 🖋

Meditation

TAKING CARE OF YOUR
FEATHERS — A BIRD'S-EYE VIEW

If you're a bird, you're constantly taking care of your thousands of feathers: preening, nibbling, bathing, and oiling them. After a long flight, you use your beak to fluff and stroke your feathers as you smooth them back into shape. When it's time to lay eggs, you build a comfortable place for them. The time you spend caring for your feathers and feathering your nest is a vital part of accomplishing your life as a bird.

You take the time to check out what's happening with your feathers. After all, your flight feathers are critical to helping you soar through the skies. Your breast feathers and downy underfeathers keep you insulated against temperature extremes, protect you from the cold, and make your nest softer.

You know that without these feathers to put you into flight, your life becomes a different reality. Imagine what it would be like not to soar above the trees, not to perch where you have a good view of everything going on, not to glide effortlessly through the clouds!

The message to us humans is clear. We need to do what it takes to care for our physical, mental, emotional, and spiritual selves. The forms of preening, nibbling, oiling, and fluffing may vary for each of us, but without some form of self-care, we may eventually find ourselves unable to soar as high or as far, or feeling "left out in the cold" without our own spiritual warmth to nurture us.

* Sit in a quiet, friendly place where you can write and think. Maybe it's your favorite coffee shop, a park bench, or your own kitchen. First, think through a typical day and a typical week in your life and make a list of ways you now "take care of your feathers."

Make an honest assessment of the time you spend just for yourself.

* Next, whether your list has three items or thirteen, make a "wish list" of at least as many additional things you'd *like* to do to take care of yourself, that you never seem to get around to trying. One way to do this is to imagine something and see if your mind immediately objects with "yes, but . . . ." If so, you'll know you're on the right track. Write down the items despite your mind's objections.

* Try one thing on your wish list each week for the next few weeks. Or structure one entire day as a "pleasure day" and do several things on the list. If this seems too "selfish," remember that self-love and self-worth are as necessary to achieving your full potential as strong feathers are to a bird's flight. Remember, too, that all birds spend time resting between flight, to restore and renew their energy.

This is a fun meditation to do with a friend. You can help each other find new ways to nurture your nests and take care of your feathers, and you can support each other in following through. 🖋

On Wings of Compassion

Maril Crabtree

SOMETIMES THE BRIDGE BETWEEN THE SEEN and the unseen is more than a feather. In this case, it was an entire bird. It was that most common and often most reviled of birds—a pigeon.

When I first saw the bird hunched in the middle of the busy sidewalk, I knew it must be wounded. As rushing feet hurried around it, its only reaction was a feeble and futile attempt to lift its wings. Mostly it sat there, eyes half-closed, breast heaving, feathers trembling.

The downtown city street was full of cars, office buildings, and people returning from lunch. I had been a guest at an exclusive luncheon club for businesswomen, and I sighed with relief as I closed the door on the high-stress, high-pressure, corporate-ladder-climbing world I had left behind several years ago. My afternoon was free to do what I loved best: writing.

But now here is this bird. I circle its trembling body and kneel in front of it a few feet away. This bird and I have formed a bond of some sort. We are the only ones who have slowed down enough to notice each other in the maelstrom of business activity.

We eye each other warily. I see no blood or other signs of injury. Its feathers look bedraggled. How long has it been there? I suspect the bird is a pigeon, one of the hundreds, if not thousands, that manage to live flying high above the business world, perching on stone ledges of older buildings, swooping down for crumbs left behind by litterers. Could it have struck a window and fallen from one of the towering buildings? Perhaps it had received a glancing blow from a car. Was it close to dying, beyond needing any help?

What to do? I've never studied ornithology, nor do I know anything about caring for wild creatures. I return to the business club where a few women linger and announce, "There's a wounded bird on the sidewalk. Does anyone know what to do?" Surely some nature-lover will step forward and take over the situation. A chorus of voices replies.

"Oh, don't touch it with your bare hands. Birds carry diseases, you know."

"Maybe the kitchen help has a paper bag you can use."

"Isn't there a Humane Society number you can call to take care of it?"

I decide to act on all suggestions. I go to the kitchen, where a kind woman washing dishes gives me a paper bag and directs me to a telephone. The Humane Society refers me to a nature center, where a voice tells me they don't handle wild birds but gives me another number to try. When I reach someone there, she asks what kind of bird it is.

"It might be a pigeon, but I really don't know."
I try to keep the querulous tone out of my voice.
"Does it matter?"

"Well, yes, it does. We only take care of birds
native to this state. Pigeons aren't considered
native."

"What do you mean? They live here year-
round. Doesn't that make them native?"

"It doesn't. For these purposes, a distinction is
made between pigeons and such wild birds as car-
dinals, jays, robins, or sparrows. Wounded pigeons
don't qualify for the special care and treatment a
cardinal would receive.

"On the other hand," the voice continues, "it
could be a dove. If it's a dove, we *could* take it. Why
don't you bring it out and we'll take a look?"

She gives me instructions on how to capture
the bird safely in my paper bag and directions on
how to reach the wildlife center, some twenty miles
south. I sigh. There goes my afternoon of writing.
Still, this wounded-bird odyssey has taken on epic
significance. I know I won't rest until I see it
through. If the wildlife center won't take it, who
knows? Maybe I'll nurse it back to health myself.

I grab the paper bag and march out to the sidewalk. No bird. It has disappeared. Frantically, I
search the area. Had it struggled into the street and
been run over? Had my hesitation to pick it up in
my bare hands meant an untimely death? Or had it
recovered from being stunned and flown away?

Disappointment and relief flood through me.

My Good Samaritan efforts are no longer needed, and I won't have to go through the intimidating ordeal of capturing and transporting a wild bird. The afternoon is mine again. Surely this is a sign from the universe that I need to hurry home and tend to my writing.

I get into my car and drive away. As I round the corner and gather speed to enter the freeway, I see a man standing on the edge of the sidewalk. He is stooped over, with scraggly hair and beard, wearing dirty clothes, weather-beaten tennis shoes, and a cardboard hand-lettered sign that says, NEED JOB. WILL WORK FOR FOOD OR $$.

I wait for the light to change. All around us swirl busy well-dressed people going to and from their busy well-planned day. His eyes are cast down, looking at the street where he has no doubt spent more than one day of his existence in recent times.

My friend Jenny carries jars of peanut butter and pop-top cans of Vienna sausages in her car for just such encounters. "I feel guilty doing nothing," she says, "but if I give money, I'll never know if it got spent on food or booze."

Maybe she's being too literal, but at that moment I wish I had a jar of peanut butter to hand out the window. All I have is an empty paper bag.

The light changes, but I find myself turning off the freeway entrance and pulling into the parking lot of a convenience store. Empty bag in hand, I wander the aisles, choosing nutritious items that don't require a can opener or cooking.

When I think of what I'd really love to eat if I'd been on my feet all day enduring sour looks or, worse, invisibility, I throw in several candy bars and a bag of chips. The total comes to $14—less than the price of the luncheon I'd just attended.

I put the bag in my car and head for the corner where I'd last seen the man. "Please, let him still be there," I find myself praying. "Don't let him disappear like the bird."

Never before had I personally responded to the homeless men who step out of the shadows to ask for a dollar or bus fare to get to some nonexistent appointment. Panhandlers, I'd labeled them: shady, shiftless characters who discovered a clever way to avoid working. Or pitiful, helpless creatures whose needs went far beyond my ability to respond. Mostly, I found ways to keep them invisible, to keep them from intruding into my preferred version of reality.

But the bird's trembling body has transformed me. If I had been willing to go out of my way—to give up a whole afternoon—to see that it got taken care of, surely I could spend a few minutes to give something to another human being. It wouldn't solve his problems in the long run, but maybe it would give him some encouragement to keep trying.

The man is still there, looking—or is it my imagination?—a little more forlorn than before. I pull over and get out of the car, carrying my bag.

"Here," I say, my own head down as I put the bag of groceries next to his ragged shoes. "I don't have a job for you, but you look like you could use some food. Good luck."

I turn to get back in the car.

"Thanks, lady."

Did I actually hear the words or is it my imagination again? I drive away fast. My heart is beating even faster. *Maybe next time,* I thought. *Maybe next time I'll have the courage to find better ways to connect—to look at him, talk to him, listen to him.* Who are we, wounded birds all, that we cannot at least pause in the midst of our daily preoccupations, and pay attention to one another in simple ways?

By the time I turn into my driveway, I'm thinking of what I'll fix for dinner, and whether I can squeeze any writing time in before preparations begin. At first, I hardly notice the half dozen or so birds perched in a row above the porch roof. Sitting still in the now-silent car, I watch as they turn toward me, dipping their wings in a jaunty salute. I can't help but wonder if "my" bird is among them. My heart returns their greeting as we fly our separate, but connected, ways into the night. ❧

Contributors

Hazel Achor finds that feathers and other spiritual connections come to her frequently as manager of a well-known spiritual consciousness bookstore in the heart of Olde Naples, Florida. Prior to moving to Naples, Hazel was an educator and counselor in California, Oregon, Colorado, and Florida. She can be contacted at Orchid Moon Bookstore, (941) 263-2535, or her e-mail address: *naplesnonnie3@aol.com.* ❧

Elissa Al-Chokhachy is a registered nurse, mother, and author of *The Angel with the Golden Glow.* Inspired by her littlest hospice patient, her illustrated children's book deeply touches the hearts of those who have experienced loss, especially the loss of a child. Through her inspirational writing and music, Elissa offers comfort, hope, and healing to the dying and the bereaved. She may be contacted at *www.worksofhope.com* or at (877) 887-2828. ❧

Paul W. Anderson, Ph.D., is a licensed psychologist in private practice and author of *Bulletproof Recovery: Stop Addiction Forever!* He writes poetry and short stories and lives in Kansas City, Missouri, with his wife, Pam, and Colonel Buddy, his Bernese mountain dog. ❧

Robert M. "Bob" Anderson, Ph.D., is human resource director for the Brown Schools Public

Education Division for the state of Texas and is president of Instructional Services, directing client companies in the areas of safety management, human resource management, quality management, and management development and training. He can be contacted at *drsbob@flash.net*. ❧

Gaylen Ariel is a teacher, a student, a journeywoman, a citizen of the Universe, and a Grandmother wisdom-keeper. She also keeps track of (and protects from wayward developers) an eagle's nest on the edge of a busy highway near her home. ❧

Amy Belanger is a professional conservation leader, presently serving as campaign director for the Southern Appalachian Forest Coalition and formerly heading the Green Party, Student Environmental Action Coalition, and Gulf Coast Environmental Defense, the group successfully battling offshore drilling in Florida. She was raised in the backwoods of North Florida (a.k.a. Southern Alabama) and has made it her mission to bring better environmental protection to the southern United States, a region whose economic hardship and political conservatism attracts destructive industries. ❧

Kara Ciel Black was born and raised just over the border from Chicago, Illinois, and has enjoyed many outdoor travel adventures including climbing, long bike trips, and long backpacks in various states and countries. Most of her volunteer work is as an "ally" to parents and young people. With degrees in education, management, and psychology, she works in human services management, is married, and lives in Seattle, Washington. ❧

A writer, dancer, and gardener by trade, **Maya Trace Borhani** comes from the Sierra Nevada foothills of Northern California, where coyote, flicker, fox, bobcat, puma, and bear infused her consciousness and experience for many years. Now residing in the San Juan Island archipelago of Washington State, she still looks to the natural world for inspiration, guidance, and renewal. The art of ritual, cultivating sacred awareness, climbing trees, and swimming in wild rivers are a few of her favorite passions in life. ❧

Antoinette Botsford works as a professional storyteller, freelance writer, and the children's editor for *The Napra ReView*. Much of her story work is drawn from her native Canadian (First Nations) heritage. She's an enthusiastic gardener, an indifferent housekeeper, loves cats and rain, kayaking, singing with the local chorale, listening to classical music, and traveling in the southwestern United States. She is hard at work on several books and creates workshops in story-related activities for people of all ages. You may contact her at *www.storybird/~rockisland.com.* ❧

Kimball C. Brooks lives with her husband in Charlotte, North Carolina. She is mother of three and grandmother of six children. She is enjoying fifteen years of sobriety and is gratefully active in a twelve-step program. ❧

Judith Christy has always lived and worked close to nature. She has worked with wildlife rehabilitation and as a cook, nutritionist, and shopkeeper. She is both a Master Gardener and a Master Composter and most recently creator of a children's garden and learning center. She lives in a hundred-year-old house with her husband and other members of an intentional community called Hearthaven. ❧

Phillip G. Crabtree grew up in western Kentucky but moved to Nashville, Tennessee, to become involved in the music industry. He has pursued a career in songwriting, recording, and playing guitar, has played for a major record label, and has independently released two CDs with his own songs. He states: "Music has always been part of my soul and life, so my heart was driven to pursue it." ❧

Cate M. Cummings is president of Cate Cummings Publicity & Promotion Group, specializing in alternative health and healing, metaphysical, New Age, spiritual, and visionary books. You may contact her at *www.bookpublicity.com*. ❧

Dr. Janet Cunningham is an internationally known board-certified specialist in regression therapy, a transpersonal counselor, seminar leader, and author. She is past president of the International Association for Regression Research and Therapies, Inc., and associate director of the International Board of Regression Therapy. Dr. Cunningham is owner of Breakthroughs to the Unconscious, a private practice in Columbia, Maryland. She has authored three books: *A Tribe Returned, Inner Selves: The Feminine* Path to Weight Loss (*for Men and Women Who Value Their Intuitive Nature)*, and *Caution: Soul Mate Ahead!*

Will Davis was born into a large family in Indian River City, Florida (now part of Titusville), and has lived there most of his life. He is an artist, counselor, and teacher. Of American Indian descent, Will is a traditional dancer and active in the Indian community where he is also known as "Talking Wolf." He attends as many powwows as he can. He also enjoys gardening, running, hiking, bicycling, camping, and eating ice cream.

Kellie Jo Dunlap is a professional bassoonist, licensed massage therapist, Reiki Master (energy healing practitioner), and sound healer. She currently lives in Naples, Florida, where she also periodically offers dream catcher workshops.

Carolyn Elizabeth is a designer who enjoys creating harmonious and beautiful spaces that reflect conscious living. She is a mother of two, an active hospice volunteer, and writer. Carolyn is currently attending "The Society of Souls," an Integrated Kabbalistic Healing School in Princeton, New Jersey. ✐

Aweisle Epstein is an intuitive psychic recluse who prefers to keep her biography to herself. You may write to her in care of her sister, **Antoinette Botsford,** whose biography appears in this section. ✐

Toby Evans is an artist, musician, and spiritual healer. She facilitates transpersonal, experiential workshops using Native American and Incan Medicine Wheel teachings. She constructed and maintains the Prairie Labyrinth near Sibley, Missouri, and is a founding member of The Labyrinth Society. ✐

Since beginning her "path with feathers," **Anna Belle Fore** has become a Reiki Master (energy healing practitioner), a Certified Spiritual Counselor, and has extensively studied energy medicine with Donna Eden, a pioneer in the field of natural energy healing. She is studying shamanism as taught by the Foundation for Shamanic Studies and has incorporated shamanic practices into her daily life and teaching. You may contact her at *anabel4@angelfire.com*. ✐

Robert Gass, Ed.D., has been known for leading-edge work in human consciousness for over twenty-five years. More than 200,000 people have participated in seminars with Robert at corporations, universities, educational centers, and conferences. He consults at the highest levels to organizations ranging from Chase Manhattan to Greenpeace, and he serves as a personal coach to business, political and spiritual leaders. Also a musical recording artist, Robert has released twenty albums with the group On Wings of Song and is coauthor of *CHANTING: Discovering Spirit in Sound.*

Laura Giess is an artist and human resources specialist who lives and works in the western Kansas city of Hays. She describes herself as "a believer always seeking the beauty and the balance within the universe, a lover of life, and a true friend." ❧

Nancy Gifford ("Mumtaz") has exhibited her art on both coasts and throughout the United States. Her assemblages (works that combine found objects with painting and sculpting techniques) have won many awards over a span of two decades. When she lived in Morocco, Nancy was given the name Mumtaz by a fortuneteller. In Persian, it means "exquisite" or "delicious." Mumtaz was also the wife of Emperor Shah Jahan, who built the Taj Mahal in her honor. Nancy believes she has received many blessings from her namesake. ❧

A Chickasaw poet, novelist, essayist, playwright, and activist, **Linda Hogan** is widely considered to be one of the most influential Native

American figures in the contemporary American literary landscape. Her writings include six volumes of poetry: *Calling Myself Home, Daughters, I Love You, Eclipse, Seeing Through the Sun, Savings,* and *The Book of Medicines.* Her fiction includes two volumes of short stories and two novels: *Mean Spirit* and *Solar Storms.* Her collection of essays, *Dwellings: A Spiritual History of the Living World,* describes her attempts to "relearn the tribal knowings of thousands of years." ❧

Debra Hooper lives in England with her husband and son and works as a clairvoyant and Reiki energy healing practitioner. She first discovered her psychic ability in early childhood. Debra also believes "in fairies and angels and happy endings." ❧

Chicago native **Greg Eric "Skip" Hultman** is a former news reporter and writer. A graduate of John Schultz's Story Workshop, he has authored many articles as both a commercial and freelance writer. As a professional naturalist, environmental writer, and illustrator, he wrote a book about native plants of the Midwest. Now living in northwestern Michigan, he is currently working on a collection of short stories and a novel that focuses on the connections between wolves and spirituality. ❧

Victoria Rose Impallomeni offers ecotours and environmental education to those who want to experience the natural water habitat of Key West and surrounding islands. She can be contacted at *www.captvictoria.com* or (888) 822-7366. ✐

K. M. Jordan grew up in Oak Park, Illinois, with her younger brother and has since lived in Wisconsin, Florida, New Mexico, and California. Her search for meaning over the past twenty years has taken her on an inner spiritual quest, which has been most gratifying. ✐

Mary-Lane Kamberg is a professional writer, author of five nonfiction books, and an award-winning poet. She is co-leader of the Kansas City Writers Group. She has a quill pen poised atop her computer desk and can be contacted at *kamberg@kctera.net*. ✐

Carolyn Lewis King is full-blooded Muscogee Creek Indian, married, with five children and four grandchildren. She is a project associate at the Haskell Indian Nations University's Youth Extension program. She comes from a family of Medicine People on her father's side of the family. On her mother's side, "we have a lot of stompdancers." She is currently enrolled as a junior at the university and plans to get a bachelor's degree in elementary education. She says, "I love life and try to live it as if I were in ceremony at all times. I want to walk a good road and leave good thoughts behind." ✐

Raven Lamoreux-Dodd began a passion for personal coaching in 1991. She contributes to a process that allows people to invest in themselves, and she finds reward in the transformation of their personal and professional lives. She has been a health care practitioner for seventeen years and traveled internationally for seven years leading seminars on personal transformation and shamanism. Raven is the director of Coach Force, Giving You the Edge, and lives with her husband on the edge of the Everglades where she can hear the owls at night. She can be contacted at *www.coachforce.com*.

Li-Young Lee, one of the world's most acclaimed poets, has published three books: *Rose, The City in Which I Love You,* and his most recent, *Book of My Nights.* He is the recipient of many awards, including the Lannan Literary Award, the Guggenheim, and the Whiting Award. He can be reached through his publisher, BOA Editions (*www.boaeditions.org*).

Lee Lessard-Tapager is an acupuncture physician and yoga instructor who dedicates her practice to meeting people where they are, with honor. She believes that there are no coincidences and that everything we encounter in life teaches us about our own divinity. Spending time in nature every day is a life-sustaining meditation for her.

Denise Linn began her spiritual journey as a result of a traumatic experience that occurred when she was seventeen years old. Shot by a sniper and left for dead, Denise had a vivid near-death experience that activated a lifelong quest to understand more about the spiritual dimension. She explored her Cherokee heritage, lived in a Zen Buddhist monastery for over two years, and spent time in many native cultures throughout the world learning healing traditions. She teaches in nineteen countries and is the author of eleven books, including *Sacred Space, Feng Shui for the Soul, Sacred Legacies,* and *Altars*. She can be contacted at *www.DeniseLinn.com.* ✌

Virginia Lore is a "Safe Nester" and sometime-psychic who shares her home with her life partner, Kevin, and her strongly intuitive daughter, Penelope. ✌

Carole Louie is a spiritual consultant specializing in the teachings of reincarnation and feng shui. She facilitates workshops and classes on interior design and feng shui, reincarnation, and spiritual growth. She can be reached at *CaroleLouie@compuserve.com.* ✌

Sheelagh G. Manheim, Ph.D., is a Jungian psychoanalyst. She has lived in the Kansas City area most of her professional life. Having grown up in the impressive natural environment of British Columbia, she has always felt like a "child of Nature" and finds renewal there. She enjoys using music, dance, and storytelling to help people express their soul. She may be contacted at P.O. Box 5852, Kansas City, Missouri 64171, (816) 753-8585. ✌

Rev. Fern Moreland has been an icon in Kansas City's dowsing and metaphysical community for many years. She is a skilled dowser, psychic reader, ghost investigator, astrologer, palmist, numerologist, teacher, ordained Spiritualist minister, and metaphysician. She has worked tirelessly to promote knowledge and understanding of the psychic arts, appearing on radio talk shows and speaking at schools, churches, and organizations. She is founder of God's Circle of Love Metaphysical Center and owner-editor of *The Good News Paper*, a local newspaper. She may be contacted at (816) 861-2575.

Mark Nepo is a poet and philosopher who has taught in the fields of poetry and spirituality for over twenty-five years. As a cancer survivor, he remains committed to the usefulness of daily inner life. He has written several books which focus on the work of inner transformation. His most recent book is *The Book of Awakening*. A collection of Mark's essays, *Unlearning Back to God*, will be published in London (Fall 2002), as well as a new book, *The Gift of Attention* (Conari Press, Fall 2003). Mark currently serves as Program Officer and Poet-in-Residence for the Fetzer Institute.

Gina Ogden is a grandmother and longtime feather enthusiast. She is also the author of *Women Who Love Sex: An Inquiry into the Expanding Spirit of Women's Erotic Experience*. Gina is now writing a book on the results of her nationwide survey, the first to investigate the emotional, spiritual, and cultural dimensions of sexual relationships. She would love to hear from you via her Web site: *www.womanspirit.net.* ❧

Pam Owens currently works as a case manager/sign language interpreter in Johnson County, Kansas. Previously she worked with deaf alcohol and drug abusers. Pam established Missouri's state program substance abuse treatment for people who are deaf or hard of hearing. She currently serves this program as a consultant. Pam also does demonstration cooking for renaissance festivals as "Mother Pockets." Her feather story was told to her by her mother, who lived in the Ozarks and was full of wonderful stories. ❧

Marty Peach is a lifelong resident of New England and leads a blessed life as the caretaker and guardian of two cockatoos and an African gray parrot. ❧

Terrill Petri is cofounder and guiding spirit of Women Vision International (WVI), a not-for-profit organization founded to improve the quality of life for women and children throughout the world by empowering women to be economically self-sufficient. WVI's efforts have included rural, grass-roots initiatives with women in Ghana, the Dominican Republic, Colombia, Zimbabwe, and the Pine Ridge Reservation of the Lakota Nation. Contact her at *www.womenvision.org* ❧

Terry Podgornik is a registered nurse who believes in the importance of caring for people as a whole, both body and spirit. She sees herself as "a small part of something much larger" and believes that "when you present yourself as spirit, wonderful connections happen." She also finds comfort and solace in nature, music, and good books. ✌

Josie RavenWing, M.A., M.F.C.C., has made the study of multicultural healing systems and spiritual paths her life's work. An internationally known workshop presenter, ceremonial leader, poet, songwriter, and author (*The Return of Spirit: A Woman's Call to Spiritual Action* and *A Season of Eagles*), Josie leads week-long Desert Visions shamanic retreats and also leads groups to Brazil several times a year to experience the work of trance medium healer Joao de Deus. She may be contacted by telephone at (954) 922-1596 or by e-mail at *jravenwing@aol.com*. Her Web site is *www.healingjourneys.net.* ✌

Rachel Naomi Remen, M.D., is the author of the bestselling *Kitchen Table Wisdom* and *My Grandfather's Blessings*, where this story first appeared. She is renowned for her work with the chronically and terminally ill. She is cofounder and medical director of the Commonweal Cancer Help Program in Bolinas, California, and is currently clinical professor of family and community medicine at the University of California at San Francisco School of Medicine. ✌

Carol Rydell is the creator of Earth Wisdom Journeys, an organization committed to teaching and supporting individuals who long for deeper meaning and purpose in their life. Through ceremony, ritual, and group experiences, Carol assists others in opening to their inner wisdom and in remembering all of who they are. She uses her love of sound and rhythm to nurture community. Carol facilitates workshops locally and internationally, gently communicating powerful messages regarding relationships to one's self, each other, and Mother Earth. You may contact her at *crydell@aol.com.*

Orazio J. Salati is an established artist and art educator living in Endicott, New York. His earlier work dealt with a specific theme, the massacre of a Native American tribe, illustrations of which are included in the book *A Tribe Returned*. Abstractions are his current expression. He may be contacted at *Buffst72@aol.com.*

Jeanne Scoville is a holistic registered nurse who has devoted over thirty years of her adult life to studying multicultural healing methodologies. She is a world traveler and a student of indigenous teachings. Jeanne deeply resonates with the elders who share their sacred oral traditions. She says, "I am at home wherever I am throughout the world, and I am personally convinced in a very organic way that we, indeed, are ALL family!"

Nancy Sena devotes her time to her main love of short story writing, after more than thirty years as a counselor for adults. She has been published in the *Miami Herald*'s *Tropic Magazine* and *The Writers' Journal.* She is active in four writing groups in the Naples, Florida, area where she and her husband make their home. ✍

Deborah Shouse is a creativity coach, writer, editor, teacher, and dreamer. She is fascinated by possibilities. Her work has appeared in *MS, Woman's Day, Family Circle, Tikkun, Reader's Digest,* and other national magazines. She is author of a number of nonfiction books and coauthor of *Working Woman's Communications Guide* and *Antiquing for Dummies.* Her work has also been published in anthologies such as *In Loving Testimony, I Am Becoming the Woman I've Wanted,* and *Chicken Soup for the Mother's Soul.* ✍

Rod C. Skenandore, Ph.D., "Elk Chief" of the Oneida/Blackfeet, is a scholar, a writer, a Sun Dance chief of long-standing, and an artist who believes that all of life is an art. As a father, grandfather, and great-grandfather, he stresses the importance of the future and is concerned with what we, worldwide, are doing in the present. He states: "We are each other's medicine, put here to take care of the sacred Mother Earth. This includes all the races. The sacred powers are our tools. We have used them for ourselves rather than for Creation. Wake up, world family, the circle is 'way out of round.' Aho." ✍

Eleanor K. Sommer is a writer and editor who lives in Gainesville, Florida. She is also an Artist-in-Residence with the Shands Arts in Medicine program where she works bedside with heart transplant patients. Her most relaxing moments are spent in her garden where she grows herbs and vegetables. ❧

Starfeather is founder and owner of Starfeather's Gallery of Sacred Art & Provisions for the Journey in Edmonds, Washington. She is a spiritual leader, visionary artist, healer, ceremonialist, writer, and teacher of creative and sacred arts. Her life is dedicated to re-establishing the Sacred Feminine on the planet, restoring balance, harmony, and respect for the Earth. Starfeather facilitates several ongoing Circles and spiritually focused retreats throughout the year. She created and performs in "In Honor of Trees" ceremonial theater. She can be contacted at *strfther@speakeasy.org*. ❧

Kenneth Ray Stubbs, Ph.D., is a certified sexologist and a certified masseur. He has given trainings in massage and sexuality throughout North America and Europe. He has also taught as an adjunct faculty member at the Institute for the Advanced Study of Human Sexuality in San Francisco and is the author of *The Essential Tantra*, *Women of the Light: The Sacred Prostitute*, and five other books on sexuality, as presented on his Web site: *www.sexandspirit.com*. ❧

Stumbling Deer is an artist and shaman. Chanting, singing, and playing Native American flute, he has led sweats, ceremonies, and vision quests for over twenty years. His pottery also reflects a Native American influence. He can be contacted at Stonesthrow Pottery, 7110 Antioch, Merriam, Kansas 66204.

Bobby Rae Sullivan was raised by her parents, Mary and Joseph Sullivan, on their ranch in southwest South Dakota on the Pine Ridge Indian Reservation. She graduated from Oglala Community School in 1972 and currently works for the Environmental Protection Agency's program of the Oglala Sioux tribe. Her parents are no longer living, and she currently lives on the original ranch east of Buffalo Gap, South Dakota, with her three daughters, three nieces, nephew, grandson, and son-in-law.

Mark E. Tannenbaum is an avid watcher of nature and believes that God's creations speak to all of us. He sees feathers as keys that unlock the doorways of the universe and provide knowledge that he shares an optimum world of peace and harmony with every creature.

Don Alberto Taxo is a Master Iachag Birdperson residing in the High Andes Mountains, named after the local *taxo* flower. In 1990 Don Alberto was appointed the highest honor by the Shamanic Council of South America and is a teacher and healer of the Cotopaxi Quichua tribe in Ecuador. He can be contacted at his Web site: *www.donalberto.org* ◆

Vickie Thompson's metaphysical path is a stark contrast to her career as an executive in the administration field. In her personal time, Vickie designs workshops that help women rediscover their "herstory" through the study of ancient goddess religions and the cultural shifts that have influenced women's lives since the advent of patriarchy. She has been writing and leading women-centered rituals for eight years. Vickie and her husband, Gary, a Reiki Master and hypnotherapist, live in Massachusetts. ◆

Gerald Wagner was born in Portland, Oregon, but grew up in Seattle, Washington. He graduated from Indian Heritage High School, received an associate studies degree from Little Big Horn College, and received a bachelor's degree from Montana State University. After working as a project coordinator for the Blackfeet Tribes Wetlands Protection program, he became director of the Tribe's Environmental Programs. His work oversees all major environmental concerns for the Blackfeet Reservations. He is also a member of the Regional and National Tribal Operations Committee. He is married, has two sons and a daughter, and states: "My family is the most important thing to me. This land is all we have and we have to do what we can to make our land a clean and healthy environment in which to raise our children." ◆

Vicki Wagoner is an area-certified hypnother-apist and a Reiki Master. She lives with her husband, Rick, and two sons, Alexander and Clinton, in Naples, Florida. 🖋

Penny Wigglesworth heads the Penny Bear Company, Inc., a nonprofit all-volunteer company that spreads messages of love, healing, and hope through gifts of teddy bears to seriously ill children and adults. Penny is also a hospice volunteer, wife, mother of four, and grandmother of seven. 🖋

Ron Yeomans lives in Kansas, "the Land of Oz," and says, "I seem to be wandering around in the wilderness with assorted witches, gargoyles, good fairies, and Munchkins. Like the Scarecrow, I have a degree and, I hope, a brain. Like the Lion, I have at least had the courage to begin my quest, but I'm not always sure where I am. Like the Tin Man, I know I have a heart because sometimes I can feel it breaking; and sometimes I can even feel love in it. Like Dorothy, I sometimes feel as though I'm not in Kansas anymore. Now and then, another feather drops into my life to show me that I'm really meant to fly, if I have the courage, the insight, and open my heart to the possibility." 🖋

Have You Had a Mystical Experience with Feathers?

IF READING THESE STORIES REMINDED YOU of your own, and you'd like to share your experience with readers for a possible future volume of *Sacred Feathers*, please send your true story to:

Maril Crabtree
3728 Tracy Avenue
Kansas City, Missouri 64105
Fax: (913) 831-4623
E-mail: *maril@prodigy.net*
or submit online at:
www.sacredfeathers.com

If you'd like to sponsor a feather workshop or reading in your region, or to be on the mailing list for dates and locations of future workshops, please contact me at the same address. Don't forget to include your name, address, phone number, and e-mail address. ✐